National Real Estate Salesperson

License Exam Prep

Ace the Exam on Your First Try with No Effort | Test Questions, Detailed Answer Explanations & Insider Tips to Score a 98% Pass Rate

Donald Pritzker

TABLE OF CONTENTS

Introduction

The path to earning a National Real Estate Salesperson license is exciting and demanding because to the complexity and ever-changing nature of the real estate industry. If you aspire to enter a field where properties become doors to dreams and deals establish links between people and places, then you need this license. The National Real Estate Salesperson License Exam is a major milestone on the path to becoming a real estate professional, so it's important to study hard and learn as much as possible about the industry.

Property ownership, value, finance, agency connections, and the many other layers that make up real estate are all explored in " National Real Estate Salesperson

License Exam Prep," your guide to passing the National Salesperson License Exam. This book is more than just a study aid; it equips future real estate professionals with a thorough understanding of the industry's fundamental concepts and practices, allowing them to not only pass the licensing exam with flying colors but also excel in their chosen fields.

The first chapter lays the groundwork for future achievement by providing essential guidance for taking the licensing exam. This chapter lays the path for future professionals by providing exam-taking advice, tactics for overcoming test anxiety, and recommendations on appropriate study approaches.

The foundation of the real estate market is property ownership. In this chapter, we'll look at the numerous ownership systems and legal descriptions that support the distinctions between real property and personal property. The many methods used to demarcate private property are explained in detail, from the traditional "metes and bounds" method to the more modern "rectangular government survey system." Additionally, the complex network of encumbrances and the investigation of air, mineral, and water rights bring to light the delicate dynamics that shape ownership.

The real estate industry relies heavily on government intervention and regulation. The impact of zoning laws, building rules, and environmental regulations on real estate development is explored in the third chapter. The precarious equilibrium between individual property rights and the needs of the larger community is explored via the lenses of historic preservation, zoning variances, and special use licenses.

Property appraisal is a crucial part of the real estate industry. In-depth discussion of valuation strategies, basic economic concepts, and market analysis are presented here. Readers will get an understanding of the methods used by licensed appraisers, including the sales comparison method, the cost approach, and the income approach to value. Readers will have the knowledge to give their clients sound advice after having investigated market tendencies, influential factors, and investment research.

Real estate financing is a dynamic and complex field. This chapter provides the groundwork for grasping the financial complexities of real estate transactions, from the breakdown of financing principles and terminology to a comprehension of the various types of mortgages and their effects. Readers will be better equipped to help clients navigate the murky waters of financing after learning about concepts like loan-to-value ratios, private mortgage insurance, and debt-to-income ratios.

The foundation of any real estate transaction is the agency connection. In this chapter, we'll examine what constitutes agency, what brokers and agents do, and how agency agreements and disclosure rules work. Readers who take the time to learn about the complexities of dual agency and conflict of interest will be better prepared to handle legal and ethical challenges in their careers.

In real estate deals, honesty must be prioritized above all else. In this chapter, we'll break down the seller's disclosure requirements, the value of doing a survey, and the state of the art in property condition disclosures. Readers learn about the effects of inadequate disclosures on real estate transactions and the possible legal repercussions that can follow.

Real estate deals can't get off the ground without contracts. This chapter allows readers to manage the complexities of offers, acceptances, contingencies, and remedies for breaches by reviewing the elements of valid contracts, knowing different contract forms, and understanding the components of real estate sales contracts.

The leasing market is a sizable component of the property market. This section clarifies the ins and outs of commercial and residential leases, including the duration of the lease, the possibility of renewal, and the respective responsibilities of the landlord and tenant. Successful leasing transactions can be facilitated by readers who have a thorough understanding of eviction procedures and the components of a lease agreement.

The key to long-term success in real estate is professional property management. Agreements for property management, standard maintenance procedures, and methods for resolving disputes are all included in this section. This chapter teaches the skills necessary for successful property management, from building rapport with tenants to handling finances with finesse.

Changes in property ownership call for in-depth familiarity with title conveyance, deeds, and title insurance. Ownership conflicts, distressed property transfers, and the nuances of closing procedures are all explained in detail. Expense proration, tax considerations, and closing cost calculations are all included in this section.

The profession of real estate is defined by open lines of communication, ethical considerations, and cutting-edge technological tools. In this chapter, we'll discuss how to effectively communicate with clients and consumers, how to manage trust and escrow accounts, the basics of fair housing law, how to effectively negotiate, and what other obligations real estate agents have. Readers will gain a thorough comprehension of their professional scope and obligations as they are introduced to ethical concerns and the legal framework governing the practice of real estate.

Real estate analysis that is reliable relies heavily on mathematical modeling. Learn the ropes of numeric analysis, financial planning, and real estate valuation with the help of this chapter! Aspiring professionals may now more easily determine monthly mortgage payments, gauge investment returns, and analyze the monetary impact of real estate deals.

The book " National Real Estate Salesperson

License Exam Prep" serves as more than just a study aid for the licensing exam; it's also a springboard to a career in the real estate industry. This study guide equips future professionals with the knowledge and confidence they need to take the licensing exam and begin their careers successfully by exploring the many facets of property ownership, financing, agency relationships, contracts, and property management. As you go out on your adventure, let this book serve as your reliable guide—a treasure trove of information that gives you the understanding, insight, and tools you need to succeed in the ever-changing real estate market.

1.

How to pass the exam

The successful completion of a crucial step along the path to earning a National Real Estate Salesperson license is contingent upon the candidate's ability to demonstrate competency on the required examination. Aspirants can use this chapter, titled "How to Pass the Exam," as a point of reference because it provides a comprehensive arsenal of methods, insights, and approaches that will allow them to navigate the exam with confidence and competence. In the pages that follow, you will find a treasure mine of useful test-taking ideas, advise on overcoming the common foe of test anxiety, and a study approach that has been painstakingly crafted in order to raise your preparation to new heights. In addition, you will find a strategy for overcoming the common adversary of test anxiety.

On the road to obtaining a license, it is not enough to simply have a firm grasp of the relevant information; you must also demonstrate an intimate familiarity with the intricacies of the field, be able to confidently react to hypothetical situations, and apply your knowledge to relevant situations in the working world. You will discover how to make the process of preparing for your exams less of a daunting burden and more of an empowering activity in this section. During this section, we are going to delve into the art of effective time management during the exam and discuss how to effectively distribute your minutes among the different questions. But that's not all; this chapter goes beyond the typical strategy by tackling a problem that isn't always discussed openly: exam anxiety. The capacity to maintain composure under pressure is a skill that can be mastered, and inside these pages, you will learn tried-and-true methods to sooth your nerves and overcome the worry that could otherwise get in the way of your accomplishments.

In addition, the study plan that is outlined in this article is not a generic prescription that can be followed by everyone; rather, it is an adaptable road map. Recognize that every student is an individual, and that in order to maximize your understanding and recall of the content, you should develop a study strategy that takes into account your preferred method of instruction, your existing skills, and any areas in which you feel you may improve. Each stage of the plan, from arranging your study resources to taking advantage of practice tests, is intended to improve your level of comprehension and memory of the topics that will be tested.

This chapter will serve as your foundation in your pursuit of a National Real Estate Salesperson License. It will provide you with a bedrock of instruction that will assist you in weathering the rigors of exam preparation. You will not only be able to conquer the problems of test-taking with the insights gained from "How to Pass the Exam," but you will also cultivate the abilities that are essential to survive in the dynamic world of real estate with these insights. Remember that passing the exam is not the goal in and of itself; rather, it is a steppingstone on the path to an exciting and rewarding profession. Therefore, enter this chapter with an open mind, a willingness to acquire knowledge, and a dedication to your own personal development. This is the beginning of your road to becoming a licensed real estate professional; get ready to do well on the test and get ready to start an exciting new adventure in the exciting world of real estate.

Test Tips:

The journey toward obtaining a National Real Estate Salesperson License is without a doubt thrilling, but it does come with a huge obstacle, and that obstacle is the licensing exam. This section, titled "Test Tips," is intended to serve as your compass, directing you through the challenging aspects of the test while also equipping you with a toolkit of ways to improve your overall performance. These test recommendations are more than just a compilation of suggestions; rather, they are carefully curated insights that draw from the complexities of the real estate market as well as the one-of-a-kind characteristics of the examination itself.

At the outset, it is absolutely necessary to acquire an understanding of the format and organization of the examination. You will be able to more effectively manage your time if you are aware of the number of questions, the amount of time allotted for each question, and the different types of questions. To acquire a better understanding, you should become familiar with the subject matter areas that will be tested on the exam. This will ensure that your preparation is both complete and focused.

Mastering the art of efficient time management is one of the fundamental pieces of advice that should be followed. The ability to allot the appropriate amount of time to each question is of the utmost importance given that the clock is ticking. We will look into strategies that may be used to evaluate the difficulty of questions and make educated decisions regarding when it is appropriate to move on to the next topic and when it is appropriate to spend more time on a specific subject. This ability not only helps you answer all of the questions within the allocated time, but it also lowers the possibility that you will spend an inordinate amount of time on difficult questions, which could hurt your overall result.

As you progress through the test, you'll come across a variety of question types, such as true/false, multiple-choice, and scenario-based questions, among others. Each format calls for a different strategy to be taken. This section provides tactics for tackling these various types of questions, educating you on how to carefully read questions, minimize distractors, and select the response that is most appropriate. These techniques have the potential to significantly improve your accuracy, which is especially important in the field of real estate, which places a premium on meticulous attention to detail.

How To Overcome Test Anxiety:

When confronted with the prospect of an examination, many people find themselves overcome with a mixture of emotions, including anticipation, uncertainty, and a racing heartbeat. Even those who have put in the most effort to prepare for an exam might still be affected by test anxiety, which can have a negative impact on performance and obscure information. The book "How to Overcome Test Anxiety" dives into the area of psychology, providing readers with insights and strategies to control anxiety and ensuring that their genuine talents are displayed during testing situations.

The first and most important step in overcoming test anxiety is gaining a knowledge of its underlying causes. The anticipation of the unknown, the dread of failing, and the pressure to do well are all factors that can lead to increased feelings of anxiety. The first step in regaining control over these triggers is to recognize them for what they are. This part provides an introduction to several mindfulness practices that serve to ground you in the here and now, removing your attention from worries about the future and making it easier for you to concentrate on the content of the examination.

In this section, we take a look at visualization, which is yet another important tool. You can prepare your mind to take the test with confidence by imagining yourself doing well on the exam. This will help you feel more prepared mentally. When you allow yourself to become completely submerged in uplifting mental images, you fill up a well of optimism that can help you combat the negative thought patterns that are connected with anxiety.

In addition to this, we go over breathing exercises, which are beneficial because regulated breathing helps biologically combat the physical signs of worry. You may control your heart rate and reach a level of calm that will help you think more clearly by practicing breathing techniques that involve deep and steady breaths.

Study Strategy:

It is without a doubt essential that you be familiar with all of the material on the National Real Estate Salesperson License Exam; but how you approach your studies is just as vital. The "Study Strategy" part is not simply about counting hours; rather, it is about improving your learning process to guarantee that you comprehend ideas, remember information, and successfully synthesize knowledge.

In this part, we argue for the importance of developing an individualized study strategy. Having an awareness of both your strong points and your weak points enables you to devote more of your time to difficult topics while more quickly going over previously covered material. The concept goes beyond merely passively reading material and places an emphasis on techniques for active learning. You can solidify your learning and improve your ability to retain information over the long term by summarizing essential points, teaching others about concepts, and participating in discussions.

The most important aspects of efficient preparation are practice tests and simulated examinations. You will become more comfortable with the format of the exam by using these tools, and you will also be able to determine which topics require more attention. In this section, you will be guided through the process of simulating exam situations, evaluating your performance, and adjusting your study plan accordingly.

In addition, the practice of creating an encouraging atmosphere for academic pursuits is investigated. These seemingly insignificant improvements, such as making your office pleasant and reducing the number of distractions in the environment, can have a huge impact on your focus and concentration. This section also looks into the impact of breaks and pace, two aspects that have been shown to reduce burnout and sustain consistent levels of production.

By applying the study strategies presented in this chapter, you can achieve your academic goals. You can improve your performance on the licensure exam as well as create skills that are transferrable to your future ventures in the real estate market if you use effective study techniques, practice active learning, and embrace a holistic approach to preparation. These three strategies are all part of an all-encompassing strategy to preparation.

These three sections—Test Tips, How to Overcome Test Anxiety, and Study Strategy—combine to offer a comprehensive toolset that prepares you for success on the dynamic journey toward getting a National Real Estate Salesperson License. Your goal is to obtain a National Real Estate Salesperson License. They are comprehensive in that they include not only the information that is necessary for the examination, but also the mental and strategic preparation that is necessary for a successful career in real estate. Keep in mind that the goal of this trip is not simply to pass an exam; rather, it is to establish a foundation of skills and information that will serve you well throughout the entirety of your adventure in the real estate industry.

2.

Property ownership

The idea of property ownership is the foundation upon which the whole real estate market is constructed, making it one of the most important aspects of this large industry. In this context, ownership is not limited to the mere act of having physical possession of anything; rather, it refers to the intricate interaction of legal rights, social dynamics, and economic factors. As we go into the second chapter, "Property Ownership," a journey of discovery opens up before us, illuminating the delicate tapestry that binds together the many facets of ownership, rights, and duties in a variety of contexts.

The key to understanding what it means to own property is to understand the difference between real property and personal property. The earlier definition takes into account not just the land itself but also everything that is connected to it, such as the buildings, resources, and minerals that lie beneath the surface. It is a tie to the soil, a stake in the terrain that carries worth, both real and intangible, for the person who possesses it. Personal property, on the other hand, refers to movable assets, such as the items that enrich our day-to-day lives; these are the kinds of possessions that go beyond simple utility to become extensions of our identities.

Nevertheless, this dichotomous classification is not the end of the story. As we delve more into the topic, the chapter reveals a variety of ownership forms, each of which has its own distinctive characteristics. Each ownership structure—from sole ownership, in which a single person exercises dominion over a property, to joint ownership models that navigate shared rights and survivorship—carries various consequences that influence decisions, inheritance, and duties. Sole ownership occurs when a single individual exercises dominion over a property.

As we progress down the path, we will soon enter the area of legal descriptions, which is a vital component in ensuring that ownership is crystal clear. The systems of metes and bounds, rectilinear government surveys, and the lot-and-block system serve as our guides, shedding light on the processes by which land borders are precisely defined and conveyed. These methods go beyond the abstract and bring legal papers to life so that they can resonate with the reality of the landscape.

However, the scope of ownership extends beyond the domain of the tangible. It embraces the resources below as well as the air above, making it a spectrum of rights that we investigate in greater depth. Understanding air, mineral, and water rights becomes crucial, particularly in the context of a quickly changing world with increased demands for resources. From the airspace that enables development and transit to the subterranean treasures that often lie buried, air, mineral, and water rights all play an important role in society.

Understanding how encumbrances, such as restrictions, liens, and claims made by third parties, interact with ownership rights is necessary in order to successfully navigate the process of property ownership. This chapter delves into the ramifications of liens, the complexities of easements, and the legal nuances of licensing in order to shed light on the intricate dance that exists between property ownership and encumbrances. These encumbrances frequently have sway over transactions, which means that they can affect both the value of the property and the transfer of ownership.

The contrast between individual ownership and shared ownership has a different impact on the physical environment. While exclusive ownership allows for unfettered individuality and decision-making authority, joint ownership necessitates collaboration and a commitment to a common goal. In situations involving law, money, and feelings, having a solid understanding of these models is absolutely necessary since they establish the parameters for cohabitation and cooperation.

Because of the complex nature of these relationships, the ownership of real estate is sometimes entangled with familial and marital ties, which led to the development of the ideas of common property and separate property. As legal systems refine their understanding of the nature of assets obtained during a marriage, the lines that demarcate individual from joint ownership of property become increasingly important. This chapter explores these facets and acknowledges the myriad of ramifications they have for couples and families.

To get to the heart of things, "Property Ownership" invites us on a journey through a terrain that fuses together legal principles, social interactions, and economic foundations. It is a symposium on rights and obligations, as well as a symposium on the essence of relationship to the land and the resources it provides. It is a symphony of the several sorts of ownership. This chapter is not only about defining terms and explaining ideas; rather, it is about giving you more control over your life. It is an invitation to understand the complexities that govern ownership, which will enable you to traverse the real estate landscape with self-assurance and comprehension. Armed with the knowledge from this chapter, you will be able to manage transactions, advise clients, and contribute to a society in which property ownership is more than just a legal framework; rather, it is a nexus of relationships, aspirations, and possibilities. As you continue through the remaining chapters, you will be able to do all of these things.

Real Property vs Personal Property:

The difference between real property and personal property is a cornerstone of real estate, affecting how ownership is viewed and how deals are structured. Land, buildings, trees, minerals, and bodies of water are all considered components of real property. It reaches up into the atmosphere and down into the ground's resources. Not only do buildings and their related legal rights fall under this umbrella, but so do plots of land themselves. Because of its physical connection to the ground, real property is generally subject to regulations governing its usage, upkeep, and taxation.

In contrast, personal property includes things that can be moved around easily. These are things that don't have to be left in one place forever and can be moved around. They might be anything from a simple piece of furniture or an expensive piece of jewelry to a car or other vehicle. In contrast to real estate, which cannot be moved or sold, personal property can be bought, sold, and traded freely among individuals.

In a wide variety of real estate situations, knowing the difference between real property and personal property is vital. Legal rights, tax ramifications, and transactional processes are all determined by whether an asset is considered real or personal property. For real estate agents to properly represent their customers' best interests during property transactions, they need a firm grasp of this distinction.

Types of Property Ownership:

The concept of property ownership is not static; rather, it includes a wide range of models that specify how title is transferred from one person to another. When one person owns something outright, that person has complete control over all management and use decisions. Conversely, in joint ownership arrangements, title is held by more than one person. In tenancy in common, co-owners possess unequal shares and are able to transfer their stake, while in joint tenancy, the surviving owner(s) immediately inherit the deceased owner's portion upon the deceased owner's passing. Only married couples can own property as tenants by the entirety, a form of joint ownership in which both partners own equal ownership and the right of succession.

Decision-making authority, transferability of ownership, and legal responsibility all play a role in ownership structure. Questions of cooperation, consent, and possible conflicts are raised by joint ownership arrangements in particular. As real estate agents help their customers through the nuances of joint ownership and related transactions, familiarity with these models is critical.

Land Characteristics and Legal Descriptions:

The distinctive properties of the land determine its value, its practical applications, and the complexities of the law that govern land ownership. Size, shape, terrain, and natural features are all examples of qualities that can be applied to a piece of land. Land value, potential for development, and other factors are all affected by these factors. The key to pinpointing an area's limits, however, is found in its legal description.

Metes and bounds is a type of legal description that uses actual measurements of a property's perimeter to establish its boundaries. This method has deep historical roots and is often used for handling oddly shaped shipments. The Rectangular Government Survey System (RGSS) is an alternative land survey system that uses townships and ranges to create a grid pattern that makes it easier to describe and transfer land in areas with consistent topography. The lot-and-block system is most used in metropolitan settings, where it is used to define property lines by referring to a recorded plat plan and thereby facilitate transactions in highly populated areas.

Surveyors, appraisers, and real estate agents all rely heavily on an accurate understanding of these features and legal descriptions of land. Property ownership, transactions, and the settlement of border disputes all rely on accurate legal descriptions. Professionals who have a firm grip on these ideas are better able to decipher legal documents, understand property boundaries, and avoid misunderstandings during real estate transactions.

Metes-and-Bounds

Recognizing property lines is only one part of comprehending land ownership; you also need to be fluent in the language of land surveys and deeds. Metes and bounds is among these instruments, and it is one of the oldest and most complex methods for legally describing land.

Metes and bounds is a system for delineating property lines that uses both straight lines and compass bearings. Typically, this method involves establishing a starting point, or "point of beginning," and then outlining the land's boundary using a predetermined set of measurements and directions. In order to ground the description in the real world, it is common practice to make use of concrete elements of the environment, such as buildings, trees, and bodies of water.

This technique has historical significance because it was used during the colonial era, when more modern surveying equipment was not readily available. When accurate measuring tools were few, it made sense to rely on landmarks in nature and established distances. For areas with varying topography or parcels with an unusual shape, metes and bounds descriptions were the best option.

Real estate agents, surveyors, and anybody else involved in land deals need a firm grasp of the metes and bounds system. The foundation of property rights and legal documents is found in precise land descriptions. Learning the ins and outs of metes and bounds helps you understand the evolution of land description techniques, value the skill of surveyors, and value permanent landmarks as reliable indicators of property lines.

The Rectangular Government Survey System (RGSS)

In the United States, it is common practice to divide land into grids for the purpose of writing legal descriptions and transferring title. The Rectangular Government Survey System (RGSS), commonly known as the Public Land Survey System, is the backbone of this network. The RGSS was first used in the late 18th century as a means of more effectively allocating and administering land in the rapidly expanding American frontier.

Each township in the RGSS is six by six miles and is divided into 36 sections, each of which is one square mile in size. These quarter-sections are subdivided into eighths, which are further subdivided into sixteenths, etc. This grid-like layout offers a standard for describing and transferring ownership of land.

In areas with relatively level terrain and surveyed land, the RGSS can be especially useful. Initially, this method was used to survey the states of Ohio, Indiana, and Illinois. It provided a methodical strategy for distributing land and facilitated the sale of public lands to settlers, who ultimately molded the American landscape.

Real estate and land development experts must be conversant with the RGSS. It makes finding, buying, and transferring property easier by providing a standardized way for legal land descriptions. Learning the RGSS's ins and outs is like getting a crash course in the evolution of land surveying and its lasting effect on the distribution and ownership of land.

Lot-and-Block system

The lot-and-block system is the dominant form of property description in dense metropolitan environments with its towering buildings and intertwined neighborhoods. Urban areas call for a more efficient and compact method to land description than the open spaces described by metes and bounds or the Rectangular Government Survey System. The documented plat map is the basis for the lot-and-block system, which simplifies property descriptions to satisfy this need.

Subdivisions are created in this way, with each lot and its boundaries specified on a plat map. Besides having distinct borders, the individual lots are identified by a specific number or letter. It is unnecessary to take precise measurements or compass readings for determining property lines if one refers to the official plat map.

The lot-and-block system functions most effectively in highly populated areas where city planning is homogeneous and efficient land description is required. To facilitate urban growth and preserve transparency in land ownership, it streamlines the property acquisition and development process.

Understanding the lot-and-block concept is crucial for real estate agents working in metropolitan areas. Accurate and smooth real estate transactions in urban areas depend on professionals' familiarity with the relationship between recorded plat maps and property transactions.

Air, Mineral, and Water Rights:

Beyond the surface of the earth, there are innumerable other potential locations for private property. When land is very valuable because of its abundance of resources or other distinguishing features, a complex web of ownership interests involving air rights, mineral rights, and water rights emerges.

The term "air rights" is used to describe the legal entitlement to the airspace above a piece of property. The ability to build upward while maintaining ownership of the land below is made possible by air rights, which become increasingly important in highly populated urban areas. It may be necessary to negotiate with adjacent property owners and comply with zoning laws in order to exercise these rights.

However, mineral rights extend into the earth's crust. Oil, gas, and minerals found on a piece of property may be subject to their own set of ownership rules. In such a case, it's possible that two or more groups will have competing legal claims to the land, with one group owning the surface while the other group holds the rights to extract the wealth contained beneath it.

When bodies of water cross property lines, the issue of who owns and who can use them becomes a legal one. These privileges may include the ability to collect rainwater in addition to the right to use surface water. In places where water is scarce or when disagreements arise over how it should be used, water rights become an important issue.

Landowners, developers, and investors who deal in areas with significant resources or special features must be aware of and respect these rights. You'll learn about the many facets of property ownership and the unique legal challenges that occur in resource-rich areas as you delve into the details of air, mineral, and water rights.

Encumbrances and Effects on Property Ownership:

When it comes to rights, constraints, and claims, property ownership is a complex notion with many points of intersection. All interests, rights, and claims that interfere with or restrict the owner's use of the property meet at this point, forming the encumbrances landscape. Encumbrances are legal claims against property that restrict its use, prevent its transfer, or expose its owner to legal responsibility.

Liens, which are legal claims placed on property as security for a debt or obligation, are a common type of encumbrance. Taxes, mortgages, and judgments all have the potential to result in liens. Until the debt is paid off, the owner may be unable to sell or transfer the property without first removing the lien.

Easements are another type of encumbrance since they allow third parties the legal right to use a piece of the land for their own benefit. Utility firms, for instance, may own easements in order to install and service utility lines that run across private land. Limitations imposed by easements may affect how a piece of property is developed.

When a piece of one property crosses into another's territory, this is called an encroachment. This may cause tensions amongst neighbors, necessitating the intervention of the law. Licenses are similar in that they allow the user to do something with a piece of property, but that use can be taken away at any time.

Real estate agents and property owners both benefit from having a firm grasp of the implications of encumbrances. Property value, marketability, and development plans are all affected by encumbrances to varying degrees. You will get a deeper understanding of the complex web of rights and constraints that governs property ownership and transactions as you investigate encumbrances and their consequences.

Liens:

Liens are an important part of the complicated system of property ownership and real estate deals. A lien is a legal encumbrance on property that affects the owner's rights to the property, the property's marketability, and the owner's access to finance.

A lien is essentially a claim against a piece of property in order to guarantee the payment of a debt or obligation. Unpaid property taxes, mortgages, or judgments are all examples of liens that can be placed on a property. Putting a lien on a piece of property makes the creditor's interest in that piece of property public record. The owner's options for selling, refinancing, or transferring the property may be limited due to this encumbrance.

Different lien forms carry different legal weight and have different repercussions. Unresolved property tax liens, the result of unpaid property taxes, can end in foreclosure. When buying property, mortgage liens are frequently used as the loan's collateral because of the value of the asset being purchased. The lender has the right to foreclose on the property if the borrower has defaulted on the mortgage.

Construction projects are the only ones eligible for mechanic's liens. If a contractor or subcontractor isn't paid for their services or supplies, they may file a mechanic's lien against the property. As a security interest, this lien gives them the right to seek for repayment.

Everyone who deals with real estate must be familiar with the concept of liens. A comprehensive understanding of liens is essential for property purchasers, sellers, lenders, and investors to make educated decisions and protect their financial interests. As you learn more about liens, you'll develop a deeper understanding of the relationship between property ownership, debt, and legal rights, which will give you more agency in real estate transactions.

Easements, Encroachments, and Licenses

Easements, encroachments, and licensing further complicate the already convoluted idea of property ownership in today's modern legal system. These guidelines strike a fair balance among property rights, neighborliness, and other legal considerations.

A legal easement allows a non-possessory third party to use real property belonging to the landowner. This could mean providing utility companies access to the property for line maintenance or sharing a driveway with a neighbor. Easements can be either permissive (allowing usage) or restrictive (limiting use), and they typically come with obligations for upkeep and adherence.

The presence of an encroachment indicates that some part of one property extends beyond the bounds of another. This is sometimes inadvertent, like when there are inaccurate surveys or a disagreement over property lines. Legal issues between neighbors over encroachments may require mediation, boundary revisions, or even litigation to resolve.

Permission to enter or use a property for a limited time and for a specified purpose is provided by a license. In contrast to easements, property owners have complete discretion over when and how to cancel permits. The act of allowing a buddy to fish in a pond on your land, for example, amounts to issuing a license. Compared to easements, which are permanent legal rights, licenses are temporary and informal.

A comprehensive understanding of property rights and legal obligations is necessary for negotiating easements, encroachments, and licensing. For the sake of legal compliance and good neighbor relations, real estate professionals, property owners, and developers should familiarize themselves with these ideas.

Other Potential Encumbrances of Title

There are several types of potential encumbrances that might affect property ownership and transactions beyond the more well defined categories of easements, encroachments, and licenses. There is a wide variety of claims, restrictions, and rights that might interfere with the transferability and value of property.

Covenants, conditions, and restrictions (CC&Rs) are a type of encumbrance commonly found in planned communities and homeowner organizations. Covenants, conditions, and restrictions (CC&Rs) establish guidelines for residents' behavior and the upkeep of their properties so that everyone can live in peace.

A property's previous owner may have imposed contractual constraints known as "deed restrictions." Property use limitations can be put in place to save natural areas, establish design standards, or limit development. They can add to the property's worth by ensuring its historic integrity is protected, but they can also restrict how the land is used.

Equitable servitudes are non-possessory interests that impose a duty on a landowner to do some action or abstain from some use of the land. For instance, a landowner may have to keep a shared pathway open or keep an established tree grove in good condition.

Real estate agents, purchasers, and sellers all need to be aware of these risks before committing to a transaction. Due diligence in real estate transactions necessitates the discovery and evaluation of such encumbrances. Whether they add to the property's appeal or place restrictions on its use, encumbrances change the dynamics of property ownership and set the terms for owners' responsibilities and privileges.

Sole Ownership vs. Joint Ownership

Property ownership models are built on the ideas of single ownership and joint ownership, with sole ownership being the most basic and joint ownership being the most complex.

One who owns a property outright has sole legal title to it. Under this arrangement, the owner has complete discretion over the property's management, improvement, and sale. While being a single proprietor has its advantages, it also puts you in the position of making all of the major financial and operational decisions.

However, in a joint ownership arrangement, title to the property is held by all of the co-owners. Different types of joint ownership structures, such as tenancy in common, joint tenancy, and tenancy by the entirety, exist. Tenants in common is a form of property ownership in which the owners hold undivided, and potentially unequal, interests in the property. The inheritance and transfer of property is made more malleable by this concept.

The right of survivorship is a legal notion made possible by joint tenancy. When one joint tenant dies, their share of the property goes to the other joint tenants automatically. This strategy eliminates the need for the time-consuming and costly probate process while ensuring a smooth transfer of ownership.

Only married couples have the legal right to hold property as tenants by the entirety, which includes the right of survivorship. This structure shields the assets of the deceased spouse from the claims of the surviving spouse.

Relationships, finances, and estate planning objectives are just some of the elements that should be taken into account when deciding between sole and joint ownership. Helping clients navigate these ownership options in a way that best suits their individual needs is a key responsibility of real estate agents and brokers.

Tenancy in Common, Joint Tenancy, and Tenancy by the Entirety

Tenancy in common, joint tenancy, and tenancy by the entirety are the three primary forms of joint ownership. There are a variety of ownership scenarios and purposes that can be accommodated by the various models, each of which has its own distinct traits, ramifications, and benefits.

When numerous people hold an undivided stake in a piece of property, the ownership structure is called "tenancy in common." Shares can be divided equally or unequally among owners, depending on the situation. Tenancy in common lacks the right of survivorship found in joint tenancy and tenancy by the entirety. This ensures that the deceased co-owner's share of the property will go to his or her descendants and not to the surviving co-owners automatically. While tenancy in common allows for more wiggle room in terms of ownership shares and transfers, it doesn't provide the same level of convenience that other models do.

The right of survivorship is a legal notion made possible by joint tenancy. When one joint tenant dies, their share of the property automatically becomes 100% owned by the other joint tenants. This strategy eliminates the need for probate by ensuring that the property ownership is instantly consolidated among the surviving co-owners. Unity of time (acquiring the property at the same time), unity of title (acquiring the property through the same deed or document), unity of interest (holding equal ownership shares), and unity of possession (having an equal right to possess the property) are the four unities necessary for joint tenancy.

For married couples, tenancy by the entirety is a form of joint ownership known as "tenancy in common." This model incorporates the "right of survivorship," which ensures that upon the death of one spouse, the other spouse will automatically take over sole ownership of the property. By holding property in joint tenancy with one's spouse, one is protected from the other's creditors. It's a sort of ownership that symbolizes the union of spouses and serves as a reflection of the marital partnership.

Successfully navigating these types of shared ownership arrangements calls for an in-depth familiarity with their subtleties and potential consequences. In counseling clients on the ownership structure that is compatible with their objectives, connections, and estate planning strategies, real estate experts play a vital role.

Community Property and Separate Property

The notions of community property and separate property within the field of property ownership dig deeply into the complexities of marital relationships, legal frameworks, and financial rights. Community property rules make these ideas all the more important.

Any assets amassed by either spouse throughout the marriage are considered community property and are owned equally by both partners. Based on this approach, spouses have an equal financial stake in all marital assets, regardless of who was responsible for their acquisition. Each spouse owns half of the community property in a community property state. In the event of a divorce or death, this model may affect how assets are divided.

In contrast, a spouse's "separate property" includes anything that person owned prior to the marriage or that person received as a gift or inheritance. Unlike community property, which is subject to equal distribution, this asset remains the sole property of the acquiring spouse. It is possible for separate property to become community property if it is combined with community property or used for the benefit of the marriage.

Couples, families, and real estate professionals all need a firm grasp of the differences between common property and separate property. It has implications for retirement planning, divorce settlements, and the financial foundations of marriage. By delving deeper into the nuances of these ownership types, you'll learn how marriage and partnerships affect property ownership in both the legal and financial senses.

3.

land Use Control Regulation

The chapter titled "Land Use Controls and Regulations" serves as a vital guide through the dense web of governmental control and societal concerns that affect the way in which we interact with land. This is true despite the fact that the real estate industry is always shifting and adapting. The concept of property ownership extends well beyond individual rights and is intricately woven into the larger social fabric, as well as the processes of environmental protection and urbanization. This chapter looks into the complex world of governmental rights and restrictions over property, covering a wide range of topics such as zoning ordinances, construction codes, environmental regulations, and historical preservation laws.

An investigation of the rights of the government to land is the focus of this chapter. This is a fundamentally important idea because it emphasizes the fundamental principle that the government possesses the inherent ability to regulate land usage for the greater good of the public. Even if people have the freedom to own their own property, the government nevertheless plays a very important part in making sure that communities are peaceful, safe, and able to continue existing.

Through the lens of zoning and zoning rules, government controls are brought to the forefront. These are mechanisms that split land into specified zones with designated permitted uses, such as residential, commercial, or industrial. These zones are then governed by zoning. These regulations seek to restrict land uses that are incompatible with one another and to preserve the character of existing communities in order to make urban planning more efficient and to reduce the likelihood of potential conflicts.

As we investigate building codes and regulations, which serve as a set of rules for safe and structurally sound construction processes, the complex relationship that exists between the government and the construction industry takes center stage. The rate of urbanization is increasing, which means that it is more important than ever to adhere to these standards in order to ensure the health and safety of residents as well as the general community.

We go into the world of environmental rules and the impact they have on real estate in light of the growing awareness about the environment that is driving policy discussions. Because the value of property and the health of the community are inextricably linked to the environment, there is a pressing need for legislation that address issues of environmental preservation, pollution, and sustainable development. To successfully negotiate these restrictions in today's real estate market, professionals are required to have extensive knowledge in order to maintain a healthy equilibrium between economic expansion and the protection of the natural environment.

This line of inquiry is expanded by the regulation of environmental hazards, which brings to light the imperative to recognize, manage, and lessen the impact of risks caused by toxins and pollutants. As concerns about the environment take center stage, professionals have been tasked with protecting both the health and safety of residents as well as the integrity of the ecosystem that is immediately surrounding them.

This chapter adds a cultural dimension by focusing on historical preservation and land use, which highlights the significance of conserving landmarks and structures that contribute to the historical narrative of a community. This chapter's main idea is that keeping landmarks and structures that contribute to a community's history is important. A nuanced grasp of the relevant legal, cultural, and economic factors is required in order to strike a healthy balance between the aspiration for contemporary growth and the requirement to protect cultural traditions.

This chapter comes to a close with a discussion of variances and special use permits, which provide a path for landowners to seek exemptions from zoning restrictions in certain circumstances where doing so is in line with the interests of the general public. These methods allow for some degree of flexibility within the legal frameworks, and they highlight the significance of adopting a flexible approach to land use management.

We develop a better understanding of the dynamic interplay between individual property rights, communal interests, environmental stewardship, and urban planning as we make our way through the complex landscape of land use rules and regulations. Real estate professionals in today's world need to have a complete awareness of the legal and sociological factors that influence how land is utilized in order to successfully navigate the difficult waters in which they find themselves. The reader will gain the knowledge necessary to become knowledgeable advocates for responsible land use, sustainable development, and harmonious community expansion if they take the time to engage with this chapter.

Government Rights in Land

The notion of government rights in land plays a fundamental part in the world of real estate, as it helps to define the parameters of property ownership and how it can be put to use. Even if the right to own property is one of the most fundamental rights, it must be exercised within the bounds of government authority in order to protect the general welfare and advance the common good. This idea originates from the antiquated doctrine of "eminent domain," which provides governments the ability to seize privately owned property for the purpose of putting it to public use, as long as the owner is given fair compensation for their loss. This authority is utilized for the construction of things like roadways, public utilities, and other forms of infrastructure.

Additionally, the government possesses the authority of police power, which enables it to make laws and regulations that promote public safety, health, and welfare. This is because the government is in possession of the power of police power. This authority is the foundation for a variety of land use rules and laws that govern property development, zoning, environmental preservation, and other areas of concern. The ability of the government to employ police power is a reflection of the delicate balance that exists between the rights of individuals to their own property and the interests of society as a whole.

Government Controls - Zoning and Zoning Ordinances

The idea of zoning and the creation of zoning rules is one of the most important aspects of the government's use of its authority to exert police power. Zoning is an essential instrument for urban planning and the regulation of land use, with the goals of preventing the use of property for purposes that are incompatible with one another and promoting the creation of an orderly plan. Zoning is a system that categorizes land into separate zones, each of which has its own set of regulations defining the kinds of uses, activities, and structures that are allowed inside that zone.

Zoning ordinances, which are the legal codifications of zoning regulations, provide an outline of the criteria for the use of land in the different zones. These ordinances address a variety of topics, including residential, commercial, industrial, and mixed-use zones, as well as considerations including building height, setbacks, lot coverage, and parking restrictions. Zoning rules play an important role in preserving the identity of neighborhoods, reducing the likelihood of traffic congestion, and maximizing the effectiveness of land use.

Building Codes and Regulations

Building codes and regulations provide a point of intersection between the world of property development and the control exercised by the government. These codes and regulations protect the safety, structural integrity, and compliance of structures with particular criteria. These regulations are intended to protect building occupants, avert potential calamities, and guarantee that all structures satisfy the fundamental standards for health and safety. The term "building codes" refers to a body of regulations that governs a wide variety of areas of construction, such as structural design, fire safety, plumbing, electrical systems, and accessibility.

There are many different stakeholders involved in the process of enforcing building codes and regulations. These stakeholders include building inspectors, engineers, architects, and contractors. Before beginning construction, developers are required to submit designs for approval that demonstrate compliance with applicable building codes. Inspections are carried out at significant points all the way through the construction process to guarantee compliance. Failure to comply with regulations may result in additional work time, financial penalties, or even the temporary halt of building until the problems are resolved.

The changes that have been made to building regulations are a reflection of the advances that have been made in technology, engineering, and knowledge regarding safety standards. They take into account not only the well-being of the building's occupants but also environmental factors such as the building's capacity to conserve energy and remain operational. The responsibility of the government to safeguard the general populace and foster conditions that improve their quality of life is highlighted by the role that the government plays in the formulation and administration of building regulations.

It is essential for real estate professionals, developers, property owners, and communities to have a solid understanding of these legal rights and restrictions imposed by the government. These methods promote orderly growth, public safety, and the maintenance of community character by striking a balance between individual property rights and greater communal interests. The ability to successfully navigate these complexities guarantees that real estate initiatives comply with legal standards and make a positive contribution to the well-being of society as a whole.

Environmental Regulations and Impact on Real Estate

Real estate and environmental issues have never been more intertwined than they are in today's world, which is characterized by rising levels of environmental knowledge and concern. The way in which properties are built, used, and transferred is significantly influenced by environmental regulations. These restrictions take into account ecological factors as well as the long-term viability of both urban and rural settings.

The regulations governing the environment cover a wide variety of subjects, including the quality of the air and water as well as the protection of endangered species and the management of hazardous waste. Different governmental entities at the federal, state, and municipal levels are responsible for drafting and enforcing these regulations. They intend to lessen the detrimental effects on the natural world, protect the natural resources that exist, and ensure the health and well-being of the communities they serve.

There are several different ways in which environmental rules might have an effect on real estate. The processes of obtaining permits to build must be navigated with great complexity by developers. These processes evaluate the projects' effects on the environment. Before land can be developed on a site with the potential for environmental contamination or sensitive habitats, it may first be necessary to undertake costly cleanup activities. In order to preserve the local ecosystems, landowners may be required to abide by regulations that restrict specific uses of their land or changes they make to their properties. In addition, prospective buyers and lenders frequently demand environmental analyses and studies in order to discover any legal responsibilities.

It is crucial for real estate professionals to have a solid understanding of environmental rules, as failure to comply with these regulations can result in significant penalties, legal responsibilities, and delays in project timetables. Recognizing the broader role that real estate plays in environmental stewardship is also a significant step in the right direction. Not only can sustainable development techniques, green building certifications, and responsible land use decisions ensure compliance with legislation, but they also contribute to the creation of a built environment that is more resilient and ecologically balanced.

Regulation of Environmental Hazards

The control of environmental risks is an essential component of both the preservation of the natural environment and the maintenance of good public health. These dangers can involve a wide variety of threats, such as contamination of the soil, pollution of the air and water, pollution of the water supply, and exposure to harmful compounds. Government agencies such as the Environmental Protection Agency (EPA) play a crucial part in the process of detecting, regulating, and reducing these risks in order to minimize harmful impacts on human health and environmental damage.

Brownfield sites, for example, are properties with confirmed or suspected contamination that impede their redevelopment. These locations are referred to as "brownfields." Brownfield sites are cleaned up and remediated under the supervision of regulatory agencies, which ultimately makes the land safe for new uses. These efforts not only bring derelict regions back to their former glory but also contribute to the economic regeneration of surrounding districts by putting vacant properties to profitable use.

Another example of a hazardous material that is subject to stringent regulations due to the link it has with a variety of respiratory diseases is asbestos. In order to safeguard the health of construction workers, tenants, and the surrounding environment, regulations specify how asbestos-containing materials must be handled, removed, and disposed of.

The oversight of potentially dangerous environmental conditions highlights the significance of conducting thorough research before to purchasing real estate. It is incumbent upon purchasers, vendors, and developers alike to carry out exhaustive environmental evaluations in order to ascertain the possible dangers and obligations that are connected to a certain property. These evaluations serve as a basis for decision-making, provide information for negotiations, and make it easier to comply with legislation governing the environment.

Historical Preservation and Land Use

Celebrating cultural heritage while also contributing to the vitality of communities is one of the goals of historical preservation, which acts as a bridge between the past and the future. The goal of both historical preservation efforts and land use restrictions is to shield historically valuable buildings, places, and landscapes from being demolished, altered, or developed in a way that is insensitive to the environment.

When it comes to the process of naming historic sites and enforcing preservation requirements, key responsibilities are played by local, state, and federal government organizations. The designation of a site as a landmark might result in financial benefits for restoration efforts in the form of tax credits and grants. However, it also establishes prohibitions on renovations that could put the historical integrity of a site in jeopardy.

The preservation of historic properties is an important factor in contributing to the one-of-a-kind personality of communities and neighborhoods. It helps to cultivate a sense of identity while also boosting tourism and making a contribution to the overall quality of life. The nuanced awareness of architectural legacy, cultural relevance, and community ambitions that is required to strike a balance between development and preservation is essential.

Variances and Special Use Permits

In spite of the fact that rules serve as a framework for land use, deviations and special use licenses make it possible to exercise some degree of creative license within these frameworks. These mechanisms recognize that specific properties and situations may depart from standard regulations while still serving the public interest. However, they are designed to do so in a way that is consistent with those standards.

When the rigid implementation of certain zoning restrictions would result in an unreasonable hardship, property owners have the ability to request exceptions through the use of variances. For example, a property owner may request a variance in order to develop closer to a property border in order to accommodate physical restrictions.

On the other hand, special use permits grant approval for specific uses that might not be allowed by right in a particular zone. This permission is granted for a specific period of time. These uses are deemed appropriate due to considerations such as the benefits they provide to the surrounding community or the limited influence they have on the neighborhood. Examples of this would be the presence of business operations in residential neighborhoods or religious institutions in residential areas.

Application, review, and public hearings are all part of the procedure for requesting either a variance or a special use permit. These procedures strike a balance between individual property rights and the needs of the society, ensuring that exceptions are granted responsibly and with an eye toward the greater good of the general populace.

4.

Valuation and Market Analysis

———————————

The search of value acts as a compass in the complex world of real estate, directing both decision-making and transactional activity. The chapter titled "Appraisal Methods and Approaches to Value" takes center stage when it comes to unraveling the complexities of establishing the worth of a property, which is a task that extends beyond simple numbers to involve economic concepts, market dynamics, and detailed analysis. Real estate professionals need to be fluent in a variety of procedures and techniques so that they can produce estimates of value that are accurate, believable, and objective. This is a landscape that they must navigate in order to succeed.

The Appraisal Methods and Approaches to Value section is the most important part of this chapter. It contains a variety of methodical techniques that can be used to determine the value of a piece of property. These approaches are like instruments that an appraiser keeps in their toolbox; they enable them to evaluate the worth of a property from a variety of perspectives. These methodologies accept that value is not a fixed idea; rather, it changes through time in reaction to changes in market trends, economic situations, and the characteristics of the property. Appraisers who have a thorough understanding of the subtleties of each method are better equipped to adjust their analysis to a wide variety of circumstances.

When one considers the function of a certified appraiser, one realizes that certain circumstances call for the knowledge of a professional educated to produce an objective and unbiased assessment of worth. This is one of the scenarios in which an appraiser is required. Mortgage financing, estate planning, legal issues, and the assessment of property taxes are some examples of these kinds of scenarios. In situations like these, the opinion of a trained appraiser becomes extremely useful because their observations serve as the foundation for making educated decisions and finding equitable solutions.

The most important part of an appraiser's job is coming up with an estimate of the property's value. The value of a property is the outcome of an in-depth research that takes into account a variety of criteria, including the characteristics of the property, its location, current market trends, and economic data. The procedure include investigating the physical characteristics of the property, evaluating its condition, and contrasting it with other properties on the market that are analogous to it. Appraisers use their knowledge and expertise to consider all of these factors and produce a precise valuation that takes into account the reality of the market.

The economic theories that underpin value in real estate serve as the foundation upon which various approaches to valuation are constructed. The appraiser's train of thought is directed by these concepts, which include supply and demand, substitution, and contribution, among others. The capacity of an appraiser to determine value and anticipate changes in market trends can be improved by increasing their knowledge of the ways in which these principles interact within the setting of the real estate market.

One of the most important approaches in an appraiser's toolkit is a comparison of recent comparable sales to the current market conditions. Appraisers make knowledgeable modifications to account for discrepancies and obtain an estimate of the property's value by evaluating recently sold properties that are comparable to the one under consideration. This strategy is based on the substitution principle, which claims that a sensible buyer would not pay more for a property than the cost of acquiring a comparable substitute. This strategy uses the principle of substitution to its advantage.

By determining the worth of a piece of property based on how much it would cost to duplicate or replace it, the cost approach provides an alternate point of view. This approach is particularly useful when dealing with one-of-a-kind or specialized properties, the value of which may be affected by the amount of money that would be required to replicate the changes.

The approach known as income analysis gets the spotlight in the case of income-generating properties. This approach investigates the potential for a property to create income by analyzing several aspects of the property, such as its rental income, expenses, and capitalization rates. Appraisers offer insights that are appealing to investors seeking returns on their investments by evaluating the revenue potential of a property.

In the midst of all of these different approaches, the process of reconciling differences emerges as an essential phase. This requires analyzing the findings gained through a variety of methods, determining their respective benefits and drawbacks, and arriving at a conclusive estimate of value that takes into account the particulars of the asset in question as well as the prevailing conditions in the market.

In addition, the Comparable Market Analysis (CMA) and the checklist that goes along with it offer real estate professionals a helpful tool that can be used to estimate the worth of a property in a manner that is less formal while still providing relevant information. CMAs are used extensively in the real estate industry to aid sellers in choosing acceptable listing prices and to assist purchasers in understanding the relative value of a property.

The chapter titled "Appraisal Methods and Approaches to Value" does a great job of introducing the reader to the complex realm of property valuation, which is a field of study that combines various analytical methods with economic principles and market tendencies. Real estate professionals have an obligation to acknowledge the complexity of the valuation process and demonstrate an adept ability to navigate valuation approaches that are tailored to a wide variety of assets, situations, and market conditions. In this chapter, readers will begin a journey to master the art of estimating value, a talent that is not only crucial for transactions but also for promoting educated and smart decision-making within the real estate landscape. As readers progress through this chapter, they will embark on a journey to master the art of evaluating value.

Appraisals Methods and Approaches to Value

Figuring out how much a piece of property is worth in the complicated world of real estate is equal parts art and science. The chapter titled "Appraisal Methods and Approaches to Value" lays forth a variety of approaches that appraisers take in order to produce precise and well-informed estimations of the value of a piece of real estate. In this context, value is more than just a collection of numbers; it encompasses the dynamics of the market, economic principles, the characteristics of the property, and analytical expertise. This chapter serves as a map for real estate professionals, pointing them in the right direction as they navigate the myriad methodologies that are fundamental to the appraisal process.

The concept of appraisal techniques, in which each method represents a different strategy for determining the worth of a piece of property, is at the center of this investigation. These approaches do not compete with one another; rather, they are complementary to one another, providing a multi-faceted perspective on value that can be adapted to a variety of contexts. The strategy that compares sales to the market, the approach that focuses on costs, and the approach that examines income are three of the most common methods.

The sales comparison and market method is one of the most important parts in an appraiser's toolkit. This strategy is predicated on the substitution principle, which holds that rational purchasers will not pay more for a property than the cost of acquiring a comparable substitute. Appraisers investigate recently sold properties in the same general category as the property under consideration, making changes to take into account any relevant variations before arriving at an estimate.

The cost approach, on the other hand, investigates the worth of a piece of property based on how much it would cost to duplicate or replace it. When analyzing features that are one of a kind or highly specialized, where the value is inextricably linked to the cost of replication, this method becomes increasingly prominent. In order to arrive at a thorough valuation, appraisers take into account a variety of criteria, including the cost of construction, the rate of depreciation, and the value of the land.

The approach known as income analysis gets the spotlight in the case of income-generating properties. At this point, attention changes to the property's potential to bring in money on its own. Appraisers take into consideration a wide range of characteristics, including capitalization rates, operational expenses, and rental income. Appraisers provide insights that resonate with investors seeking returns on their investments by evaluating the revenue potential of a property.

Situations Requiring a Certified Appraiser

In a number of real estate transactions that call for an impartial and objective valuation estimate, the part that a licensed appraiser plays becomes increasingly important. This function goes beyond just determining the market value of a piece of property, as licensed appraisers are qualified to offer insights that form the basis for important choices. Real estate disputes and transactions can include a wide range of scenarios, each of which may call for the specialized knowledge of a qualified appraiser.

Certified appraisers play a crucial role in the process of determining the value of a piece of real estate that is going to be utilized as collateral for a loan in the industry of mortgage financing. For the purpose of ensuring that the loans they provide are commensurate with the value of the property, lenders rely on appraisals that are correct. This valuation serves as a preventative measure against either over- or under-financing the project.

In the process of estate planning, certified appraisers make a contribution to the fair distribution of assets by determining the assets' current fair market value. This evaluation guarantees that inheritances are distributed in a just manner and that estate taxes are computed in an exact manner. In a similar vein, professional appraisers offer a voice that is impartial and authoritative during the process of assessing the worth of marital assets during the proceedings of a divorce.

In the event of a legal issue, such as one involving eminent domain, it is necessary to enlist the services of qualified appraisers in order to estimate the worth of the assets that are up for grabs by governmental organizations. In situations like these, these appraisers play an important role in ensuring that property owners receive fair recompense for their holdings.

Estimating Value

Estimating value is the most important step in the assessment process. This is a complex endeavor that combines elements of both art and science. This attempt is far more complex than simply crunching numbers; it calls for an in-depth grasp of the property, its characteristics, the surrounding market, and the economic concepts that determine value.

An in-depth examination of the property's physical characteristics is essential to arriving at an accurate estimate of its value. Appraisers take into account a variety of criteria, including condition, size, layout, and the quality of the structure. The value of the property can be pieced together from its various components in this way.

The dynamics of the market also exert a significant amount of effect. Appraisers analyze the supply and demand for properties that are comparable in the market, looking for trends and changes that may have an effect on the value of the property. The appraiser's line of reasoning is guided by economic principles such as substitution, which proposes that purchasers will not pay more for a property than the cost of purchasing a comparable substitute. This idea suggests that buyers will not spend more than the cost of acquiring a comparable substitute.

In addition, the process of appraising a property adheres to the idea of contribution, which acknowledges that particular aspects of a property might have an outsized influence on the property's worth. A property's desirability and value can be considerably increased by the addition of features such as a swimming pool, a view, or a kitchen that has been thoughtfully planned.

The process of estimating value includes other steps as well, such as reconciling the results obtained using the various approaches. To arrive at a conclusive estimate that takes into account the complexities of the property as well as the current state of the market, appraisers do a painstaking analysis of the results acquired from various methodologies.

Economic Principles of Value in Real Estate

A profound relationship that is the basis for property valuation is revealed by the complicated dance that takes place between economics and real estate. Real estate assessments are constructed from the ground up using the idea of economic principles of value as the basis upon which they are built. When appraising real estate, appraisers must navigate the complicated environment, taking into account market dynamics, consumer behavior, and the fundamental forces of supply and demand. These principles, which are rooted in economic theory, serve as a roadmap for appraising real estate.

The principle of substitution is the fundamental idea that rational buyers and sellers will make decisions based on the availability of comparable alternatives. It is at the center of these economic concepts since it postulates that rational buyers and sellers will make judgments. This principle has a strong bearing on real estate valuation, and it suggests that a buyer would not pay more for a property than the cost of acquiring a similar property with features that are comparable to those of the property being purchased.

The concept of contribution holds that specific features of a piece of property contribute a disproportionate amount to the overall value of the asset. The appeal of a house, and hence its worth, can be considerably impacted by the addition of amenities such as a swimming pool, a kitchen that is tastefully constructed, or a spectacular outlook. Appraisers give careful consideration to each of these contributions and analyze the ways in which certain improvements influence the overall value of a property.

A further extension of economic concepts is the principle of anticipation, which states that value is impacted by an individual's expectations of the benefits that will be gained in the future. Buyers evaluate properties with an eye toward the future, taking into account factors such as the possibility of appreciation, rental income, and forthcoming trends. The complicated relationship that exists between the current state of the market and projected value is brought to light by this principle.

Sales / Market Comparison Approach

The sales/market comparison approach is one of the most important tools in an appraiser's toolbox since it exemplifies both the substitution principle and the supply-and-demand dynamics. This strategy is consistent with the old cliché in real estate that "no two properties are exactly alike." As a result of this, appraisers investigate recently sold properties that are comparable to the property under consideration in terms of dimensions, geographical location, overall condition, and specific characteristics. These other properties, which together are referred to as comparables or "comps," serve as a standard against which the value of the property in question can be determined.

An organized procedure is followed by the sales comparison method. This procedure entails identifying appropriate comparables, compensating for variances, and arriving at an estimated value. Variations in criteria such as lot size, number of bedrooms and bathrooms, square footage, and condition are all taken into consideration by adjustments. Appraisers perform painstaking research on each of these aspects to provide an objective comparison and precise evaluation.

The core of value that is driven by the market is reflected in the sales comparison approach since it is aligned with the principle of substitution. It identifies the preferences of buyers and sellers in the current market climate, illuminating the price range in which a sensible transaction is likely to take place. This information is gathered from the market as a whole. This strategy is especially important in residential real estate, where the one-of-a-kind nature of each individual home necessitates a comprehensive analysis that takes into account both similarities and differences among the properties.

Cost Approach

The cost technique provides an additional channel for evaluation in circumstances when specialized renovations or one-of-a-kind properties are in question. A property is valued using this method by determining how much it would cost to recreate or replace it. This method takes into account the value of the land as well as the cost of making improvements. It is presumptive that a sane buyer would not pay more for a piece of real estate than it would cost to buy the land and build a property that is comparable to the one being purchased.

The cost approach investigates a number of different components. The first factor is the cost of the land, which may be calculated by looking at the most recent transactions of land parcels that are equivalent to one another in the area. The second part of the process entails determining the total cost of the renovations, which include both the buildings and the physical alterations made to the site. This requires performing an analysis of the cost of construction while also taking into account depreciation caused by factors like as age, wear and tear, and obsolescence.

The cost method places a significant emphasis on depreciation, which can be broken down into three distinct categories: physical degradation, functional obsolescence, and external obsolescence. The gradual wearing away of a property's structure and contents due to the passage of time is referred to as its "physical deterioration." The term "functional obsolescence" refers to aspects of a product's design or characteristics that have become obsolete or ineffective. On the other hand, external obsolescence is brought on by elements that are not associated with the property itself, such as alterations that take place in the surrounding area or the conditions of the economy.

When all of these aspects are taken into account, the result is an estimate of the worth of the property based on the cost approach. The cost approach is particularly useful for valuing assets that have distinguishing features, but it also adds valuable insights to other valuation approaches, which makes it easier to conduct an all-encompassing study that takes into consideration a variety of points of view.

Income Analysis Approach

The income analysis approach is one of the distinct pillars that can be found within the mosaic of real estate appraisal methodologies. This approach is particularly pertinent to properties that provide income. Taking this perspective will allow you to see a world in which the worth of a property is tightly related to its potential to generate money. Appraisers acquire insights that appeal with investors seeking returns on their investments when they investigate the financial aspects of real estate.

The concept of capitalization, which is a process that converts the predicted future income that a property will provide into its worth at the present time, is at the core of the income analysis methodology. This process shows the investor's desire to earn a return on their investment that is proportionate with the level of risk they are assuming. Consequently, this goal is reflected in the process. The capitalization rate is the most important variable in the capitalization equation. This rate is expressed as a percentage and illustrates the correlation between a property's net operating income and its market value.

The approach of calculating income uses net operating income, abbreviated as NOI, as a foundational component. It is comprised of the revenue that the property generates less its operational expenses, except any expenses that are tied to the mortgage on the property. The net operating income (NOI) of a property sums up its potential earnings by taking into account variables including rental income, vacancies, and operational expenses.

Capitalization rates are not always the same and can change depending on factors such as the state of the market, the preferences of investors, and the inherent dangers associated with a particular piece of property. They reflect the investor's perceptions of risk and embody the investor's expectations for returns on their investment. A lower capitalization rate indicates a higher level of risk, whereas a higher rate indicates a higher level of risk.

The income analysis method is utilized by appraisers in the valuation of a wide variety of revenue-generating properties, ranging from hotels and apartment complexes to commercial and industrial spaces and multi-family dwellings. It is necessary to have a comprehensive awareness of each category's particular property type, market trends, and income sources in order to succeed in that category. Appraisers can contribute to a more dynamic real estate landscape by adopting the income analysis technique, which enables them to make informed investment decisions and facilitates an environment in which value is synonymous with income potential.

Reconciliation - A Final Estimate of Value

The time of reconciliation presents itself as a critical crossroads for appraisers as they make their way through the complex maze of valuation procedures. Appraisers must go through a procedure known as "reconciliation" before arriving at a conclusive value estimate. This involves comparing and contrasting the results that were acquired through the various approaches to valuation. It is a fluid process that calls for shrewd judgment, analytical dexterity, and a profound familiarity with the subtleties of the property and the market.

The idea that several approaches provide various points of view on the worth of a piece of property is at the heart of the reconciliation process. Appraisers can offset the constraints of individual approaches and arrive at a value estimate that incorporates a wider spectrum of characteristics if they reconcile various viewpoints, which are different ways of looking at the same thing. This procedure accepts the idea that there is no one way that can completely capture the value of a piece of property, and that all of the methodologies add a different component to the overall picture.

The results that are obtained via the sales/market comparison strategy, the cost approach, and the income analysis approach are analyzed and scrutinized by appraisers. They take into account the advantages and disadvantages of each strategy, taking into account aspects such as the one-of-a-kind nature of the property, the tendencies of the market, and the availability of data. The conclusive estimate of worth is arrived at as a result of conducting such a detailed investigation, with the appraiser's knowledge and professional judgment serving as guides.

Comparable Market Analysis (CMA)

The Comparable Market Analysis, or CMA, is a technique that real estate professionals can use to estimate property values in a manner that is less formal than an official appraisal but that is nevertheless instructive. This tool is distinct from formal appraisals. Real estate brokers frequently utilize comparative market analyses, or CMAs, to aid sellers in choosing acceptable listing prices and to assist purchasers in understanding the relative value of a property.

In order to perform a comparative market analysis (CMA), you will need to locate properties that are analogous to the one you are analyzing in terms of size, location, condition, and attributes. These comparables, which are also referred to as "comps," offer insights into current market patterns and the price range within which the subject property is expected to sell. Comparables are also referred to as "comps."

When real estate agents are prepared with a CMA, they are able to provide their clients with insightful information. When it comes to price, a CMA acts as a guide for sellers, helping them strike a balance between maximizing their returns and enticing possible purchasers. A comparative market analysis (CMA) makes it easier for purchasers to make educated decisions by assisting them in determining whether the asking price of a property is reasonable or whether there is opportunity for negotiation.

CMA Checklist

A systematic CMA checklist acts as a compass that directs real estate professionals through the process of completing a Comparable Market Analysis (CMA), which is a process that is notoriously difficult to carry out. The use of this checklist emphasizes the significance of conducting exhaustive research, gathering precise data, and conducting careful analysis.

Typical items on the checklist for a CMA are the identification of comparable properties, an analysis of the subject property's condition and attributes, a review of recent sales data, and an adjustment for variations between the subject property and the comparable properties. This highlights the need of having an in-depth knowledge of the local market trends, economic data, and external factors that may have an effect on property values.

Real estate professionals are urged to apply rigorous critical thinking and analysis by following the steps outlined in the checklist, which prompts them to analyze the influence of factors such as the property's location, size, layout, and amenities. In addition, it highlights how important it is to deliver the findings of the CMA to clients in a way that is both clear and transparent, as this helps to develop trust as well as decision-making that is informed.

Real Estate Market Trends

As the real estate market evolves, experts, investors, and consumers look to market trends as a reliable guide. Property values, buyer behavior, and investment strategies are all affected by market trends because they shed light on underlying patterns, movements, and dynamics. By keeping up with these developments, real estate agents and brokers may better comprehend the factors that drive the market and make calculated moves in an increasingly complex environment.

The dynamics of supply and demand are reflected in the prevailing market trends. In a seller's market, where demand exceeds supply, property values rise. When supply is higher than demand, however, prices tend to fall, creating a buyer's market. Beyond raw numbers, these tendencies encompass economic indicators, consumer attitude, and extraneous factors that affect the real estate market.

Factors that Influence Market Trends

Real estate market trends are not formed by a single component but rather represent the convergence of a number of variables. Economic indicators, interest rates, demographic shifts, and outside events all play a role in shaping market movements.

Gross domestic product (GDP), unemployment rates, and other economic indicators all have significant impacts on the direction of markets. Strong employment and wage growth can boost home demand and push up prices. However, economic downturns can undermine confidence and curb spending because of the accompanying uncertainty.

The market can be affected by changes in interest rates. Since reduced interest rates make mortgage payments more manageable, they often increase demand. However, increased borrowing costs due to higher interest rates can have a depressing effect on demand.

Changes in the population's demographics have substantial sway. For instance, the influx of millennials into the housing market has altered tastes and increased demand for properties like urban apartments and entry-level houses. The need for retirement communities and handicapped-accessible homes has also risen as a result of the country's aging population.

The real estate market can be affected by a wide variety of external factors, from geopolitical tensions to natural calamities. Demand for housing, in turn, can affect property values as a result of factors such as big corporate relocations or the expansion of local industries.

Buyers' and Sellers' Market

Real estate activity cycles between periods of extremely high demand and extremely low demand, giving rise to the two distinct market conditions known as buyers' markets and sellers' markets.

When supply is more than demand, buyers have the upper hand in a market. Sellers become more amenable to bargaining when their listings sit for prolonged lengths of time. In many cases, buyers are able to save money since they have more bargaining leverage and more options to choose from.

On the other hand, when demand exceeds supply, as in a sellers' market, prices tend to rise. Multiple offers are not uncommon, and properties generally sell rapidly for prices close to or even higher than the asking price. There is more rivalry among buyers and less willingness on the part of sellers to lower their asking prices in such a market.

Numerous variables, such as stock on hand, interest rates, and economic indicators, contribute to the current state of the market and its relative favorability to either buyers or sellers. Experts in the field of real estate are able to adapt their plans to the ever-changing conditions of the market.

Investment Analysis and ROI Calculation

Besides providing a roof over one's head, real estate is a good place to put money. Investment analysis was born out of the need to understand the complex relationship between a building's market value, rental income, and operating costs. Investors can use the results of this analysis to predict the profitability of their property purchases.

The profitability of an investment can be quantified by calculating its return on investment (ROI). It provides a numeric representation of the correlation between investment gain and investment expense. Return on investment (ROI) in real estate involves calculating the net profit after deducting the costs of owning and operating the property, including management fees, repairs, taxes, and mortgage payments.

Capitalization rate (cap rate) and cash-on-cash return are two more terms that play a role in the study of investments. The capitalization rate is proportional to the ratio of NOI to the value of a property. Increasing the cap rate increases the return potential, but it also increases the risk. When calculating the return on an investment, cash-on-cash ratios compare the investment's cash flow to the capital outlay.

Investors consider not only the property's ability to generate income and appreciate in value, but also the prevailing market conditions. Investment potential is affected by factors such as a property's location, the property's condition, and the local rental market dynamics.

5.

Financing

———•———————————•———

The chapter on Financing acts as a guiding compass through the labyrinth of real estate transactions, showing the numerous channels that connect property dreams to physical ownership. This chapter also serves as a resource for anyone interested in real estate investing. It reveals the intricate web of financial systems that, when put into place, enable individuals to close the gap between their dreams and their actual lives. This chapter covers a spectrum of issues that highlight the central role that financing plays in the world of real estate. These topics range from the fundamental concepts and terminology that drive financial debates to the crucial function that financial institutions play in changing the landscape of real estate. It reveals the procedures that enable buyers to obtain houses, investigate a variety of possibilities for mortgages, and negotiate the legal and regulatory framework that controls these types of transactions. This chapter equips readers with the knowledge and insights necessary to navigate the complex world of financing in real estate by delving into the complexities of property ownership, exploring the intricacies of mortgage structures, and revealing the legalities that underpin financial arrangements. Additionally, this chapter reveals the legalities that underpin financial arrangements. The purpose of this investigation is to provide readers with the knowledge and resources necessary to engage in profitable real estate transactions, make well-informed judgments, and capture opportunities, all while having a full understanding of the financial foundations that propel the real estate business ahead.

Financing Concepts and Terminology

In the complex environment of real estate transactions, having a solid foundational understanding of the numerous finance concepts and terms that form the road to property ownership is essential to establishing a solid foundation for one's knowledge. These phrases serve as the threads that weave the complex tapestry of mortgages, interest rates, and financial agreements. They also serve as the terms that dictate the conditions of interaction between buyers, sellers, and lenders.

The concept of interest rates, which establish the fees associated with taking out a loan to buy a home, is the driving force behind this industry. These rates, regardless of whether they are constant or variable, play an essential part in the process of shaping the financial landscape, both in the near term and in the long term.

The down payment is an important initial investment made by the buyer toward the overall cost of the property. This payment impacts the total loan amount, the amount that must be paid each month, and the probability of requiring private mortgage insurance (PMI).

Because the length of the loan determines the total amount that must be paid back each month, it is crucial to comprehend the terms of the loan. Although longer periods could result in cheaper monthly payments, they could also lead to greater overall interest charges over the course of the loan.

The steady lowering of the loan balance over time that occurs as a result of making regular payments is illustrated by the principle of amortization. This procedure assures that a portion of each payment is applied toward both the interest and the principal of the loan, which ultimately results in the loan being repaid in its whole.

The term "equity," which refers to the difference between the current market value of a property and the amount still owed on the mortgage on that property, has emerged as an essential component of financial analysis. Homeowners have a greater sense of financial stability as a result of the gradual accumulation of equity that results from making mortgage payments over time.

In the realm of real estate financing, the utilization of collateral refers to the placement of a property that acts as a guarantee for the payment of the loan. In the event of a default, the lender has the right to assert ownership of the collateral in order to recoup their losses and get their money back.

Credit scores are a significant factor that goes into deciding the conditions attached to a loan.

These numerical representations of creditworthiness have an effect on the interest rates that are made available by lenders, with higher scores leading to more favorable terms.

A technique for keeping monies for property-related expenses, such as property taxes and homeowners insurance, can be accomplished through the use of escrow accounts. This makes certain that these monetary responsibilities are satisfied, which is to the benefit of both purchasers and lenders.

It is absolutely necessary to have a solid understanding of these ideas and terminology when working in the field of real estate financing. Buyers and sellers may negotiate the negotiation process with confidence, make decisions that are based on accurate information, and enter into property transactions with a crystal clear understanding of the financial framework that underpins their undertakings when they are armed with this knowledge.

Property Ownership - Who Holds the Title

When it comes to the landscape of property ownership, the subject of who has the title is of the utmost importance because it not only implies legal rights but also carries with it personal aspirations, financial duties, and the possibility of legal problems. The complexities of property ownership can be dissected in order to shed light on the myriad of forms it might take as well as the repercussions that result from each form.

The most basic type of property ownership is called "sole ownership," and it refers to the situation in which just one person is responsible for all of the property's legal responsibilities. Individuals benefit from this structure because it grants them autonomy in decision-making and the ability to handle the property in whatever manner they deem appropriate.

Joint ownership, on the other hand, introduces the concept of shared ownership, in which two or more people hold an interest in the property jointly. Tenancy in common or joint tenancy are two options for structuring this kind of arrangement.

Tenancy in common permits co-owners to hold unequal parts of the property and permits each co-owner to leave their inheritance to their heirs upon their passing. This structure is adaptable, so it can take into account a variety of monetary contributions.

The right of survivorship is included in the joint tenancy arrangement, which requires co-owners to have equal ownership shares. This ensures that if one co-owner goes away, their share of the property will be automatically transferred to the owner(s) who are still alive.

Tenancy by the entirety is a special type of joint ownership that can only be held by married couples. Only married couples can own tenancy by the entirety. It gives protection against the creditors of each individual spouse and includes the right of survivorship.

The ideas of separate property and community property both come into play in the states that have passed legislation establishing community property. The assets that are considered community property are those that were obtained during the marriage, whereas the assets that are considered separate property are those that were acquired prior to the marriage or through inheritance.

It is known as the title, and depending on the form of ownership, it can be held in a variety of different ways. The title is the legal instrument that establishes ownership rights. Aspirants to property ownership absolutely need to have this level of nuanced knowledge, because it gives them the ability to negotiate the complexity of property ownership with clarity and self-assurance.

Pre-Qualified vs Pre-Approved

In the world of real estate, the phrases "pre-qualified" and "pre-approved" have quite different connotations, and these differences can have a considerable influence on the way in which a property is purchased. These phrases distinguish between various levels of monetary preparedness and serve as crucial checkpoints on the path to becoming a homeowner.

The purpose of pre-qualification is to perform an initial evaluation of a buyer's financial standing to determine whether or not they are qualified to obtain a mortgage. At this point in the process, potential buyers give a lender with some fundamental financial information. The lender then provides an estimate of the loan amount that the buyers would be eligible for. Pre-qualification provides a general picture of one's financial situation but does not ensure that a loan will be approved.

Pre-approval, on the other hand, refers to a process that is more in-depth and involves a more in-depth analysis of a buyer's current financial situation. The buyer is required to provide comprehensive financial data throughout this process, which gives lenders the opportunity to undertake an in-depth investigation on the buyer's credit history, income, and current debts. Lenders will make a commitment to lend a particular amount once pre-approval has been granted, but this commitment is reliant upon the borrower satisfying a number of requirements.

The difference between being pre-qualified and having your loan pre-approved is an important one for purchasers to understand. While pre-qualification will give you an initial idea of how much house you can buy, pre-approval will give you an actual promise from the lending institution. A letter stating that a buyer has been pre-approved for a loan enables them to confidently make bids on houses, negotiate successfully, and expedite the process of purchasing a home.

Underwriting

The process of underwriting, which serves as the financial backbone of real estate transactions and plays a critical role in determining whether or not mortgage loans are viable, acts as a key gatekeeper. This painstaking review guarantees that both the lenders and the borrowers enter into agreements with a crystal-clear awareness of their respective financial capabilities and obligations.

Lenders do an analysis of the borrower's financial health throughout the underwriting process. This analysis involves looking at a variety of indicators, including the borrower's credit history, income, employment stability, and existing obligations. The purpose of this evaluation is to determine whether or not the borrower can successfully juggle their mortgage payments together with their other financial obligations.

Loan-to-Value (LTV)

The idea of loan-to-value, abbreviated as LTV, is an essential metric in the world of real estate financing. Its purpose is to bridge the gap between the worth of a property and the amount of financing that purchasers are looking for. This percentage is extremely important in determining the terms of mortgage loans, and it has an impact not only on borrowers but also on lenders when it comes to the goal of property ownership.

The loan-to-value (LTV) ratio is a measurement that attempts to quantify the relationship that exists between the amount of the loan and the value that was placed on the property. The loan-to-value (LTV) ratio would be 80% in the above scenario if the appraised value of the property was $300,000 and the borrower requested a loan of $240,000. Because a larger LTV ratio indicates a higher degree of exposure in the event of default, this ratio is a powerful indication of risk for lenders.

The loan-to-value (LTV) ratio is a metric that lenders use to evaluate the possible risk that is connected with a mortgage. A lower LTV ratio indicates that the borrower has a greater equity position in the property, which acts as a buffer against financial loss in the event that the property is foreclosed upon. On the other side, a higher LTV ratio indicates that the equity cushion is smaller and that there is a greater possibility of financial loss for the lender in the event that the borrower defaults on the loan.

Private Mortgage Insurance (PMI)

When the loan-to-value (LTV) ratio of a borrower is greater than a specific threshold, which is often somewhere around 80%, the idea of private mortgage insurance (PMI) comes into play. Lenders have a layer of security against the possibility of incurring financial losses thanks to private mortgage insurance (PMI), which works as a precaution in the event that borrowers fail to make their mortgage payments.

When the loan-to-value ratio goes above 80%, private mortgage insurance (PMI) is typically demanded of the borrower because it indicates that they have less equity invested in the property. Borrowers will incur an additional expense as a result, which will be added to their regular mortgage payments. The price of private mortgage insurance (PMI) shifts in accordance with a number of variables, including the sum of the loan, the borrower's credit score, and the amount of money put down.

Even though private mortgage insurance is largely beneficial to lenders since it lowers the amount of risk they are exposed to, it also offers advantages to borrowers. Borrowers are able to acquire mortgage financing with a reduced down payment thanks to private mortgage insurance (PMI), which might potentially speed up the path to homeownership. In addition, homeowners who continue to make payments on their mortgage and create equity may eventually be eligible to request the cancellation of their private mortgage insurance (PMI) after the loan-to-value ratio falls below 80%.

Debt-to-Income (DTI) Ratio

The Debt-to-Income (DTI) ratio emerges as a crucial indicator that shines light on an individual's financial health and capacity to manage extra financial responsibilities in the complex web of real estate financing. This ratio measures how much of an individual's income goes toward paying off debt. This ratio is a measurement of the proportion of an individual's income that goes toward the payment of debt. It provides information on an individual's ability to manage mortgage payments in addition to other financial commitments.

A person's DTI can be determined by dividing the whole amount of their monthly debt payments by their total monthly gross income. This leads to the calculation of a percentage that represents the proportion of revenue that goes toward paying off debt. For example, the DTI ratio would be 30% if an individual's monthly debt payments was $1,500 and their gross monthly income was $5,000. This would indicate that the individual's debt-to-income ratio was 30%.

When determining whether or not a potential borrower is qualified for a mortgage loan, lenders place a significant emphasis on the DTI ratio. It is generally agreed upon that having a debt-to-income ratio that is lower is preferable, as this demonstrates a greater degree of financial flexibility. It is common practice for lenders to establish maximum DTI ratio criteria in order to ensure that borrowers have the ability to meet all of their financial commitments, including mortgage payments, without falling behind.

Principal, Interest, Taxes, and Insurance (PITI)

The essential elements that make up a mortgage payment are encapsulated in the acronym PITI, which stands for "Principal," "Interest," and "Taxes and Insurance." The financial commitments that homeowners take on as they negotiate the world of property ownership are built on this tetrad of components, which serves as the foundation of those commitments.

The percentage of the monthly mortgage payment that is applied directly toward reducing the total amount still owed on the loan is referred to as the principal. The principal amount is reduced with each monthly payment, which results in the homeowner's equity being steadily built up over time.

The cost of borrowing money from the lender is represented by the interest that is charged. Both the interest rate and the amount of principal that is still owed on the loan have an effect on the interest part of the mortgage payment. When first starting out on a mortgage, a greater amount of each payment will go toward the interest on the loan.

Property taxes are included in taxes and are levied by municipal governments. These taxes are typically collected by the lender as part of the monthly mortgage payment, and they make a contribution to the provision of community services and amenities. The tax payments are subsequently sent to the appropriate government agency by the lender.

Insurance refers to homeowner's insurance, which protects a person's property and the things inside it against financial loss in the event of damage. Similar to how taxes are handled, homeowners' insurance premiums are frequently collected by the lender and then forwarded to the insurance provider on the homeowner's behalf.

When added together, the PITI components make up the entire monthly mortgage payment. This payment gives an all-encompassing view of the financial obligations that come with being a home owner. This all-encompassing perspective guarantees that homeowners are well-equipped for the upcoming financial journey by enabling them to comprehend how their cash should be allocated for the purposes of accumulating equity, making debt payments,

47

paying taxes, and protecting their investment.

When the veil is lifted from the complexities of Loan-to-Value (LTV) ratios, Private Mortgage Insurance (PMI) ratios, Debt-to-Income (DTI) ratios, and the anatomy of mortgage payments through Principal, Interest, Taxes, and Insurance (PITI), the landscape of real estate financing becomes a terrain of informed decisions, strategic planning, and a steadfast understanding of the financial foundations that underpin property ownership.

Escrow Accounts

Escrow accounts have emerged as a vital tool that adds a layer of financial responsibility and transparency to the process of transacting real estate, which is a complex and convoluted industry in and of itself. The smooth transfer of payments, taxes, and insurance premiums between buyers, sellers, and lenders can be facilitated with the use of these accounts, which serve as custodial repositories for the cash.

When a real estate deal is being closed, it is customarily done so in conjunction with the establishment of an escrow account. It fulfills the role of an intermediary, keeping funds in reserve until certain conditions are satisfied. When acquiring a home, for instance, a buyer may be required to make a deposit into an escrow account in order to pay for future costs such as property taxes and homeowner's insurance. After that, the escrow agent will distribute these monies to the relevant parties at the proper times, such as when payments are due.

How Mortgage Interest is Paid

The idea of paying interest on a mortgage is a fundamental part of the real estate financing process, and it highlights the expense involved in borrowing money from a lender. When a homeowner makes their monthly mortgage payment, some of that payment goes toward paying off the loan's principal amount, while the remaining payment goes toward paying off the interest that has accumulated.

The interest on mortgages is often paid in arrears, which means that a greater amount of the initial installments goes toward paying off the principal balance. As time goes on, a greater proportion of the payments goes toward paying down the principal of the loan. This structure reflects the way lenders limit their risk by collecting a major percentage of the interest up front, and it is structured like this because of the way that lending works.

Calculating Mortgage Payments (Principal + Interest)

Unraveling the tangled web of a mathematical tapestry is an analogy that comes to mind when attempting to comprehend the process of calculating mortgage payments. These payments, which include both the principal and the interest components, are the lifeblood of property ownership and represent the core of duties with regard to one's financial situation.

Mortgage payments are often computed with the assistance of a formula that consists of the principal amount borrowed, the interest rate, and the period of the loan. The result of applying this formula is a predetermined amount that must be paid on a monthly basis by the homeowner for the duration of the loan.

However, within the confines of fixed-rate mortgages, a phenomenon that is rather remarkable takes place. While the amount paid each month does not change, the proportion of payments made toward principal versus interest does change over time. A greater portion of the monthly payment goes toward the payment of the interest on the mortgage during the first few years of the loan. As the loan matures, the proportion of the payment that goes toward the reduction of the principle steadily increases.

Mortgage Points

Borrowers have a fascinating opportunity to have some control over the interest rates attached to their mortgages by taking advantage of mortgage points, which are also known as discount points and loan origination points. Borrowers have the opportunity to get a reduced interest rate by paying an upfront fee at the time of closing in the form of "points," which are effectively a type of prepaid interest.

The cost of one mortgage point is typically equal to one percent of the total loan amount. Borrowers can effectively "buy down" their interest rate by purchasing points, which leads to reduced monthly payments throughout the life of the loan and a lower total amount paid back. Because the upfront investment in points can lead to large interest savings over time, this strategic strategy can be particularly favorable for long-term homeownership.

Types of Mortgage Loans

The realm of real estate financing offers borrowers a wide variety of mortgage loan options, each of which is tailored to meet the unique requirements, financial profiles, and long-term objectives of individual borrowers. Buyers get the ability to make informed judgments that are in line with their goals when they have a solid understanding of the available possibilities.

Fixed-rate mortgages, in which the interest rate is locked in at the beginning of the loan and does not change during its life, are one of the most frequent types of mortgages. Because of this consistency and its ability to provide predictability, it is a popular option among homeowners.

On the other hand, adjustable-rate mortgages, also known as ARMs, have interest rates that change on a regular basis, typically after an initial fixed period of time. ARMs have the ability to give lower starting rates, but they also have the risk that the rates will rise over the course of the loan.

Mortgages backed by the government, such as those provided by the Federal Housing Administration (FHA) or the Department of Veterans Affairs (VA), provide access to finance for persons who may not qualify for standard loans owing to credit or financial limits. These individuals may be able to take advantage of government-backed mortgages.

In addition, specialist mortgage products such as jumbo loans are designed specifically for the financing of expensive real estate, while interest-only mortgages give borrowers the opportunity to pay only the interest on their loans for a set length of time before the loan becomes fully amortized with principal and interest payments.

Government-Backed Loans

In the convoluted web of real estate financing, government-backed loans emerge as a cornerstone that supports accessibility to homeownership for persons who may have difficulty in securing traditional loans. This makes it possible for these individuals to own homes even though they may have trouble obtaining traditional loans. These loans, which are backed by federal agencies, serve a crucial role in creating inclusion and enabling a varied variety of persons to begin the journey toward home ownership. They also play a part in reducing the overall cost of the mortgage.

The Federal Housing Administration, more commonly known as "FHA," is a significant player in the market for loans backed by the government. The Federal Housing Administration (FHA) provides loans that are intended to assist first-time homeowners, as well as those with weaker credit ratings or inadequate finances for the down payment. The insurance provided by the agency reduces the risk for lenders, making it more likely for them to provide finance to borrowers who might not otherwise satisfy the requirements for conventional loans.

In a similar vein, the Department of Veterans Affairs (VA) offers possibilities for active-duty service members and military veterans to get mortgages with preferential terms and frequently without the requirement of making a down payment. Because the VA guarantees loans to lenders, eligible borrowers no longer need to obtain private mortgage insurance, which results in a reduction in their overall financial obligations.

In order to encourage homeownership and foster economic growth in underrepresented communities, the United States Department of Agriculture (USDA) also plays a role by providing loans in rural and some suburban areas.

Other Types of Loans

The panorama of real estate financing extends far beyond the world of traditional and government-backed loans to embrace a wide variety of different sorts of loans that are tailored to individual circumstances, financial goals, and property characteristics. These loans are available in the marketplace. Borrowers benefit from the individualized solutions that these specialty loan products offer, which are crafted to meet their specific requirements.

Conventional loans have a cap on the amount that can be borrowed, but jumbo loans have far higher thresholds, so they can accommodate houses with much higher prices. These loans give borrowers access to finance for more expensive houses; nevertheless, they typically need greater down payments and adhere to stricter credit requirements.

Borrowers can take advantage of the flexibility offered by interest-only mortgages to pay just the interest on their loans for a certain amount of time, which is often the first few years of the loan's term. Although this structure results in reduced initial payments, it is extremely important for borrowers to be aware that their payment obligations will increase once the interest-only phase of the loan comes to an end.

Mortgages known as balloon mortgages have smaller regular payments for a predetermined amount of time, followed by a higher "balloon payment" obligation at the end of the loan's term. Because the borrowers of these loans need to be ready to handle the balloon payment when it becomes due, careful consideration and planning are required before applying for one of these loans.

Bridge loans are short-term financing solutions that are designed to assist homeowners in closing the finance gap that exists between the sale of their present property and the purchase of their next home. The financial flexibility they enable during times of transition may be offset, however, by the often higher interest rates and fees associated with these loans.

Primary Mortgage Market

The main mortgage market is a bustling nexus that brings together borrowers and lenders to facilitate the exchange of money that are necessary for the completion of property transactions. This market serves as the first point of contact for borrowers who are looking to acquire mortgage loans in order to support their aspirations of owning real estate.

There are several different types of lenders in the primary mortgage market, including online lenders, credit unions, mortgage brokers, and traditional banks. Borrowers negotiate this environment by completing loan applications, presenting financial paperwork, and going through credit assessments in order to establish whether or not they are eligible for funding.

The relationship between lenders and borrowers is essential to the primary mortgage market since lenders base the terms and interest rates of mortgage loans on the borrower's creditworthiness, as well as the stability of the borrower's income, and the value of the property. This market also provides a wide variety of loan products to meet the needs of borrowers with a variety of different types of financial profiles.

Secondary Mortgage Market

Mortgage loans can be bought, sold, and traded within the secondary mortgage market, which is a dynamic domain that exists outside the realm of the primary mortgage market. This market is comprised of investors and financial institutions. Because of the role that this market plays as a conduit for boosting liquidity, it enables lenders to free up capital and generate a greater number of loans.

The Federal National Mortgage Association (Fannie Mae), which buys mortgage loans and packages them into mortgage-backed securities, is one of the key players in the secondary mortgage market. These mortgage-backed securities can then be sold to investors. After that, these securities are sold to investors, who are given the option to participate in a diversified pool of mortgages through the purchase of these securities.

In a similar manner, the Federal Home Loan Mortgage Corporation, also known as Freddie Mac, is active in the secondary mortgage market. It does this by purchasing mortgages and then securitizing them in order to increase both stability and liquidity within the housing finance system.

By having an impact on the supply and demand dynamics of mortgage-backed securities, the secondary mortgage market is an essential component in both the formation of interest rates and the accessibility of mortgage financing. Borrowers are able to gain access to finance, and investors are able to strategically distribute their capital because to the fluidity of the flow of capital that is maintained by this interconnected web of primary and secondary markets.

Security Instrument Clauses

As the real estate financing process unfolds like a complicated symphony, the terms in the security instrument emerge as essential notes that are integral to the harmonious connection that exists between lenders and borrowers. These clauses, which are included in mortgage agreements, detail the terms and circumstances that serve to protect the lender's interest in the property while also providing borrowers with the opportunity to realize their dreams of becoming homeowners.

A mortgage or deed of trust, both of which function as a type of legal contract that transfers ownership of the property to the lender in exchange for the loan, are examples of common security instruments. This instrument comprises a number of terms that control the obligations of the borrower and the rights of the lender in the event that the borrower defaults on their commitments.

Foreclosures

Homeownership is a goal that many people strive for and a desire that many people have, but the harsh fact is that unexpected financial difficulties can lead to the upsetting scenario of foreclosure. As a result of the borrower's failure to fulfill their duties regarding the mortgage, the lender may initiate the legal procedure known as foreclosure in order to reclaim title of the property.

The steps involved in the foreclosure process can be different from one state's laws and one form of security instrument to another. Nevertheless, the procedure usually consists of a number of stages, such as the default, the notice of default, the auction or sale, and sometimes the eviction. It is imperative for homeowners who are experiencing financial issues to investigate several alternatives to foreclosure, including as loan modification, refinancing, or short sales, in order to lessen the potential damage on their credit and their overall financial well-being.

Financing and Credit Laws

The sphere of real estate financing is supported by a complex web of regulations governing financing and credit that are intended to assure openness, fairness, and prudent lending practices. These statutes include restrictions that encourage access to credit, maintain the stability of the financial system, and shield borrowers against tactics that are considered to be unfairly exploitative.

The Truth in Lending Act (TILA) is a significant piece of legislation because it requires lenders to disclose essential information to borrowers, such as interest rates, terms of the loan, and any fees associated with the loan. Borrowers are given the ability to make educated decisions about their loans and evaluate the actual cost of borrowing as a result of this.

The Equal Credit Opportunity Act (ECOA) was enacted with the intention of putting an end to discriminatory lending practices that were motivated by characteristics such as a person's color, gender, religious affiliation, or marital status. This ensures that all people have equitable access to the various credit options that are available.

The Home Mortgage Disclosure Act (HMDA) mandates that lenders disclose information regarding mortgage applications, including whether or not the applications were approved. This data helps uncover potential inequalities in lending processes, which ensures that fair lending regulations are followed and helps assure compliance.

Qualified Mortgages

The notion of qualifying mortgages shines as a light of prudent lending practices within the sphere of real estate financing. A qualifying mortgage is a specific kind of loan that satisfies the requirements that have been set forth by the Consumer Financial Protection Bureau (CFPB) for the purpose of ensuring that borrowers are in a position to pay back the money they borrow.

A debt-to-income ratio of 43% or less, limits on risky loan features, and protections that defend borrowers against exorbitant fees and points are some of the criteria that must be met for a mortgage to be considered eligible. Mortgage lenders who provide qualified borrowers with loans are afforded legal protections against borrower allegations of unfair lending practices.

Creative Financing Strategies

Individuals are able to negotiate the complexity of property acquisition and investment with inventiveness because to unique financing methods that are utilized in the arena of real estate transactions. These creative financing strategies serve as a canvas upon which innovative solutions are painted. These tactics go beyond the conventional means of obtaining funding since they provide choices that can be adapted to the specific conditions and objectives of the investor.

One such method is known as "seller financing," in which the person selling the property takes on the role of the lender and provides the buyer with a loan. This arrangement may be beneficial for purchasers who are unable to qualify for conventional loans as well as for sellers who are looking to attract a larger pool of potential buyers.

Tenants have the ability to rent a property with the opportunity to purchase it at a predetermined price after a specified length of time under the terms of a lease-to-own arrangement, which provides another innovative path. This strategy gives renters the chance to create equity in their homes while also providing them time to improve their overall financial status in preparation for a future purchase.

A buyer can use a tactic known as "assumption of mortgage" to take over the current mortgage that the seller has on the property. This can be useful in situations where the terms of the seller's mortgage are more advantageous than the market rates that are currently available.

The process of creating a new mortgage that "wraps around" an existing one is referred to as a wraparound mortgage. The payments are made to the seller, who then continues to make payments on the initial mortgage. The buyer makes payments to the seller. Buyers that have difficulty obtaining conventional finance may profit from utilizing this strategy.

Role of Financial Institutions in Real Estate Transactions

Financial institutions emerge as essential players in the intricate web of real estate transactions, providing the monetary infrastructure that propels property acquisitions, investments, and overall economic growth. This is accomplished through providing loans, mortgages, and other forms of credit. These institutions include a wide variety of financial service providers, including conventional banks, credit unions, and online lenders, as well as mortgage brokers.

By providing borrowers with a variety of loan products that can be used for the acquisition of property as well as for refinancing, banks are an integral part of the real estate ecosystem. They act as middlemen between depositors and borrowers, lending out the money that has been placed by clients in order to finance the operations of both private persons and commercial enterprises.

Credit unions are financial institutions that function very similarly to banks, except they are often owned by their members and put the requirements of those members ahead of maximizing profits. They frequently provide their members with highly competitive interest rates in addition to individualized care.

Mortgage brokers function as middlemen between borrowers and lenders, assisting borrowers in locating loan options that are appropriate for their circumstances and linking them with lenders who are able to meet their funding requirements.

The traditional methods of obtaining loans have been significantly altered by the advent of online lenders, who provide shortened procedures and faster access to funds. Individuals that prioritize convenience and engaging in activities online are likely to seek out these lenders.

When it comes to the secondary mortgage market, investment banks play an important role by purchasing and securitizing mortgage loans for the purpose of reselling them to investors. The liquidity and effectiveness of the mortgage market are both improved because to their involvement.

Individuals have the possibility to engage in real estate without directly owning properties through the use of real estate investment trusts, which are abbreviated as REITs. Real estate investment trusts (REITs) are companies that invest in, manage, or finance income-producing real estate and then pay dividends to their shareholders.

6.

General principles of Agency

—————•—————

The chapter named "General Principles of Agency" is the star of the real estate industry's convoluted terrain, as it lays bare the dense network of relationships, duties, and ethical considerations that underpins the complex world of real estate transactions. When it comes to the purchasing, selling, and representing of real estate, the concept of agency is fundamental. Fiduciary duty, contractual agreement, and open communication all find their place in this dynamic framework that includes agents, clients, customers, and consumers.

The chapter's core contrast is between agency and non-agency connections. On the one hand, agents have a special duty of loyalty and trust to their clients and must always look out for their clients' best interests. Non-agency connections, on the other hand, provide a narrower sort of representation by emphasizing provision of minimal aid rather than comprehensive advocacy. Each party's familiarity with this distinction determines the nature of the assistance and obligations that will be present throughout a transaction.

There are three main types of people who interact with agencies: clients, customers, and consumers. There are varying degrees of commitment and accountability required for each position. Agents owe their clients a fiduciary duty to look out for their best interests, guaranteeing them the finest degree of representation possible. Consumers and customers alike engage in transactions without being represented by an agent, even though they may receive some level of support. The relevance of these responsibilities and the weight of their ramifications are explored in this chapter.

The wide variety of real estate agents just adds to the richness of the tapestry. Agents can either represent the vendor, the buyer, or both parties. Specific roles and responsibilities for each agent type are discussed in length. The difference between a real estate agent and a broker is also clarified, as are the relative functions and contributions of each in a real estate transaction.

Agents' duties to their principals form the moral backbone of agency relationships. Fiduciary duties include loyalty, secrecy, and complete disclosure, and are owed by agents acting on behalf of clients. These responsibilities guarantee that the needs of the clientele are prioritized at all times. However, the duties owed to clients place a greater emphasis on expert guidance and open communication, albeit to varying degrees.

Establishing agency agreements becomes a turning point in the agency system. To protect everyone's interests, it's crucial to select an agent, define responsibilities, and put the agreement in writing.

The need for openness in the field of agency work cannot be overstated. The role of agency disclosure laws in this context is clear. All parties to a transaction must be informed of any agency relationships under these laws. Because of this transparency, everyone can make educated decisions about who is responsible for what.

The chapter discusses the two main types of agency contracts: listing contracts and buyer agency contracts. Buyer agency agreements define the agent's duty in supporting the buyer throughout the buying process and are distinct from listing agreements, which provide agents the authority to promote and sell properties on behalf of sellers. Contractual duties are examined alongside the nuanced nature, variety, and constituent parts of such agreements.

This chapter guides you through the complex landscape of ending an agency relationship. The same way that an agency relationship can begin, it can also end. It is crucial for all parties involved to have an understanding of the terms under which an agency partnership might be ended.

The chapter concludes by discussing the thorny ethical idea of dual agency and the attendant problem of conflict of interest. When an intermediary acts as agent for both the buyer and the seller, a situation known as "dual agency" exists. Potential conflicts of interest are raised, and agents must carefully balance their duties to both parties in this situation. This chapter provides agents with the knowledge they need to handle complex circumstances with ease by discussing ethical considerations and methods for reducing the likelihood of conflict.

The chapter titled "General Principles of Agency" digs deep into the complex web of interdependencies, responsibilities, and functions that make up agency in the real estate industry. This chapter presents a thorough analysis of the fundamental concepts that govern the relationships between agents, clients, customers, and consumers, from comprehending the many degrees of representation to understanding the fiduciary obligations that come with agency.

Agency vs Non-Agency Relationships

Making a clear difference between agency partnerships and non-agency relationships is of the utmost importance while negotiating the complexities of real estate transactions. In agency partnerships, there is an elevated level of commitment and fiduciary duty, as agents are tasked with representing their clients in a manner that is in their clients' best interests. When acting in this role, agents advocate for their clients, negotiate on their behalf, and make choices in order to fulfill their clients' requirements.

On the other hand, non-agency interactions are distinguished by the provision of aid that is more constrained in scope. In this context, agents provide services that make the transaction easier to complete, but they do not participate in the same level of advocacy as they do in agency partnerships. The provision of fundamental information and assistance with administrative responsibilities are common components of non-agency relationships. However, unlike agency relationships, non-agency partnerships do not assume the comprehensive responsibilities that are associated with agency relationships.

Clients, Customers, and Consumers

The roles of clients, customers, and consumers all carry significant significance within the landscape of the agency industry. Clients are individuals or entities that have signed a formal agreement with an agent to act as their agent in some capacity. This agreement lays the groundwork for the agent's fiduciary duties and stipulates that they must always act in the client's best interests.

On the other hand, customers are those who seek assistance from an agent but have not established a formal agency connection with that agent. Even though agents still provide helpful information and support to consumers, they are not subject to the same duties of loyalty and confidentiality that they would be if they were working with clients.

Consumers are a distinct category in the real estate industry since they conduct transactions on their own without the assistance of a representative of any kind. Without the assistance of an agent, these people must rely on their own knowledge and abilities to conduct research and negotiate. It is crucial for agents to understand these roles so that they may correctly adjust the services they provide and the duties they take on based on the requirements and expectations of each party.

Types of Agents

The realm of real estate contains a wide variety of different kinds of agents, each of which has a unique set of functions and obligations. One typical type is the seller's agent, who acts only in the seller's interest throughout the transaction. In addition to representing the interests of the seller, these agents are responsible for marketing the property, facilitating the process, and negotiating offers.

On the other hand, buyer's agents are experts in looking out for the purchaser's best interests throughout the entirety of the buying process. As part of their job, they are responsible for assisting purchasers in locating houses that meet their needs, negotiating offers, and navigating the complexities of contracts.

When a single agent, known as a dual agent, represents both the buyer and the seller in a transaction, it can create an interesting and potentially lucrative scenario. Because of the nature of the situation, it is necessary to strike a careful balance between the responsibilities of each party and their level of openness in order to protect the interests of both parties.

It is also necessary to have a solid understanding of the distinction between a broker and an agent. Agents and brokers both play significant roles within the sector, however brokers are often in charge of the day-to-day operations of agents. Brokers have additional training and duties, such as managing a group of agents and ensuring that they are acting in accordance with the law and ethical standards.

Agent vs. Broker Roles and Responsibilities

The tasks that agents and brokers play and the obligations that they are responsible for play a key role in the complex world of real estate, affecting the landscape of transactions, negotiations, and client contacts. In the process of facilitating real estate transactions, agents and brokers each play an important part; nevertheless, these roles are distinct from one another in terms of the required credentials, responsibilities, and overall control.

An individual who has satisfied the prerequisites for education and licensure in order to operate as a client's representative in real estate transactions is referred to as a real estate agent. They perform their duties under the direction of a broker and are frequently the first point of contact for clients among the industry specialists. Agents are responsible for a variety of activities, including creating contracts, assisting customers with negotiations, exhibiting properties, and providing information about the market.

A broker, on the other hand, is a more senior-level professional who has completed further training and licensing requirements, and who might also have more experience working in the sector. Brokers are permitted to manage their own real estate businesses and may employ agents to work under their direction in the event that they choose to do so. They frequently have the right to operate on their own, which enables them to handle a variety of responsibilities, such as managing agents and reviewing transactions. Some of them even own and run their own brokerage firms.

Agent Responsibilities to Clients and Customers

A set of obligations that ensure ethical and professional behavior govern the relationship that exists between agents and their clients and customers. These responsibilities guide the relationship that exists between agents and their clients and consumers. Agents owe their customers fiduciary duties, which include loyalty, secrecy, complete disclosure, obedience, and reasonable care. Fiduciary duties also involve reasonable care. These responsibilities highlight the agent's dedication to providing comprehensive representation to their clients and working for the best interests of their customers.

When it comes to customers, agents have an obligation to offer information that is true and transparent; however, the fiduciary duties that are owed to customers are not as comprehensive as those that are owed to clients. Agents are obliged to continue adhering to professional standards, upholding honesty, and providing support to clients as they navigate the process of either buying or selling a home.

Establishing Agency Agreements

Establishing agency agreements is one of the most important elements in developing a successful agency relationship. The formalization of the connection between a client and an agent through the use of these agreements includes the assignment of duties, responsibilities, and obligations to each side. The transaction process is often guided by these agreements, which are typically established in writing and serve as a road map.

Agency agreements often detail the responsibilities of both parties, as well as the scope of representation, the length of the partnership, the agent's income, and the longevity of the relationship. These agreements are necessary because they provide clarity and transparency, hence lowering the likelihood that there will be misunderstandings or disagreements further on in the process of the transaction.

Agency Disclosure Laws

Both transparency and disclosure are essential components of an ethical real estate operation, and this is especially true with regard to the agency disclosure rules that govern the industry. These regulations are different in each country, but in general, they compel real estate agents to reveal their agency relationship to everybody and everyone who is a party to a real estate transaction. It is important to make sure that everyone is aware of the agent's position and responsibilities in order to facilitate decision-making that is based on accurate information.

Written agreements and specific disclosure statements are two examples of common types of agency disclosure. These forms of disclosure are used to inform clients, customers, and consumers about the nature of the relationship. The ultimate goal is to avoid any potential conflicts of interest and make certain that all parties are aware of who is acting as a representative for whom during the transaction.

Listing Agreements

When it comes to the business of real estate transactions, listing agreements play the role of the groundwork upon which a property is promoted and ultimately sold. These agreements provide a legal partnership between a seller and a real estate agent, describing the terms and conditions under which the agent would promote and sell the property on behalf of the seller. This relationship is established through the signing of one of these agreements.

Listing agreements provide specific information about essential aspects of the transaction, such as the period of the agreement, the agent's responsibilities, the commission that the agent will receive, and the listing price of the property. These contracts are available in a variety of formats, and each one may be adapted to satisfy the requirements and inclinations of the seller as well as those of the agent.

A sole listing agreement confers exclusivity on a single agent, which means that during the time period stipulated in the agreement, only that agent is authorized to represent the property. A broad listing agreement enables the seller to work with more than one real estate agent to market the property; the commission is paid to the agent who is ultimately successful in finding a buyer for the home.

Buyer Agency Agreements

In the same way as listing agreements delineate the working connection between sellers and agents, buyer agency agreements formally establish the working relationship between purchasers and the agents of their choice. These agreements provide clarity regarding the responsibilities of the agent when it comes to supporting the buyer, including assisting them in the search for properties that meet their needs, negotiating offers, and navigating the complexities of the process.

There are two possible types of buyer agency agreements: exclusive and non-exclusive. The buyer is restricted to working with only one agent under the terms of an exclusive agreement, but under the terms of a non-exclusive agreement, they are free to deal with more than one agency. Agreements on the representation of buyers by agents, regardless of the form they take, lay the foundation for a cooperative and fruitful working relationship between purchasers and agents.

Termination of Agency

Circumstances may at times emerge that call for the termination of agency partnerships. In these cases, the relationship must be severed. The procedure for terminating the agency relationship should be fully stated and understood before it can be done, regardless of the reasons for doing so—whether it be a shift in the circumstances, a divergence in expectations, or a desire to collaborate with a different agent.

The parties involved in the transaction can terminate the agency relationship by reaching an agreement to do so, the transaction can be closed out, or the time of the contract can run out. On the other hand, things can get more complicated if one of the parties wants to end the agency partnership earlier than expected. In situations like these, it is absolutely necessary to stick to the terms that are described in the listing or buyer agency agreement. Such agreements typically contain rules for notice periods and processes for termination.

Dual Agency and Conflict of Interest

In order to successfully navigate the treacherous waters of dual agency, one must have a solid awareness of the potential conflicts of interest that may occur. When one real estate agent represents both the buyer and the seller in a single transaction, this is known as dual agency. Although this can make communication and negotiating more efficient, it also makes it more difficult to remain unbiased and to look out for what's in the best interests of both sides.

Agents who find themselves in situations involving dual agencies have a responsibility to favor open communication and transparency. They are obligated to tell both parties of their dual agency status and have their informed consent before moving forward with the transaction. It is of the utmost importance to manage any potential conflicts of interest in a cautious manner and to make certain that both the buyer and the seller are aware of their rights and the choices available to them.

7.

Property Disclosure

The idea of property disclosures takes on utmost relevance in the field of real estate, which is a place where aspirations and realistic considerations collide and where dreams and investments often go hand in hand. Transactions involving real estate include much more than merely the passing of title to a piece of property; rather, they involve a nuanced dance between knowledge, intents, and duties. This chapter looks into the diverse world of property disclosures, shining light on the role that they play in creating transparency, minimizing risks, and ensuring that informed decisions are made in the real estate sector.

Properties are more than just a collection of walls and floors; they are rich with history, opportunity, and the beginning of a new chapter in the buyers' life. Disclosure of the property condition goes beyond superficial looks and provides a thorough picture of the property's physical situation. It takes into account not only the outside appearance of the property but also its structural soundness, its operating systems, and its general health as a whole. Disclosures regarding the condition of the property allow sellers to present a truthful portrayal of the state of their own property, which in turn provides purchasers with the information they need to make well-informed decisions that are in line with their requirements.

In the case of real estate, the scope of ownership is determined by the boundaries of the property, the structures that are located nearby, and the characteristics of the ground itself. Property surveys are the guardians of this context's cartography, serving to delineate property lines, easements, and encroachments. Property surveys help buyers understand the physical scope of their investments by providing them with accurate measurements and graphical representations of the property boundaries. This reduces the likelihood of future boundary conflicts. The spatial complexities that affect a property's worth and how it is put to use can be conveyed through surveys, which help bridge the gap between imagination and reality.

A variety of disclosures regarding properties are required by law in most legal jurisdictions in an effort to promote openness and equity. These contain a broad range of information, ranging from possible environmental dangers to flood zone classifications and all in between. Disclosures of this kind are intended to supply purchasers with vital information that may influence the choices they ultimately make. Disclosures regarding the property that are required are essential procedures that protect the rights of buyers and help to prevent future conflicts. This helps to ensure that buyers go into deals fully informed and prepared.

The seller has the moral obligation to provide complete and accurate information regarding the history of the property as well as its current condition. This obligation sits at the heart of all real estate transactions. The disclosure statement provided by the vendor is a demonstration of their dedication to being as open and honest as possible. This paper summarizes the known flaws, repairs, and other important particulars, providing prospective buyers with the information they need to make educated decisions that are in line with their tastes. The duties placed on sellers to disclose relevant information are a cornerstone of ethical real estate practices that promote honesty and reliability within the sector.

Disclosures regarding the property serve as the foundation upon which real estate transactions are constructed. They equip buyers with the ability to make judgments based on a comprehensive grasp of the qualities of a property, including both the positive and the negative aspects of the property. Disclosures that are erroneous or incomplete might lead to uncertainty, which can be a source of tension during talks and even possible legal obstacles. The effect of disclosures is felt throughout the entirety of the transaction, having an impact not only on the discussions and pricing dynamics but also on the overall level of trust that exists between buyers and sellers.

The decision to conceal facts about a property or to give inaccurate information about it might have significant repercussions. It is possible to open the door to disagreements, legal lawsuits, and financial liabilities by withholding relevant information or failing to reveal recognized problems. Inadequate information may result in unanticipated issues for purchasers, which may have an impact on the value or usability of the property. Because of the dangers connected with concealment, maintaining honesty and openness throughout the disclosure process is of the utmost significance.

Inadequate property declarations have the potential to set off a domino effect of legal entanglements and disagreements. If a buyer discovers undiscovered flaws or dangers, they have the right to seek remedies, such as the termination of the contract or financial reparation. The failure to disclose all relevant information may give rise to allegations of fraudulent behavior, violation of contract, or misrepresentation. When sellers fail to fulfill their disclosure responsibilities, they run the risk of becoming embroiled in legal processes, which can result in detrimental effects to both their finances and their reputations.

This chapter sheds light on the complex realm of property disclosures and illustrates how they serve as vital pillars of ethical real estate practices. Property condition, surveys, required disclosures, and the responsibilities of the seller all merge to create a landscape that is driven by transparency and mutual confidence in the transactions that take place. In the end, property disclosures serve as the conduit between hopes and realities, ensuring that the journey of buying or selling a property is defined by fairness, authenticity, and an unshakable dedication to well-informed judgments. This is done by ensuring that the journey of buying or selling a property is characterized by the property disclosures.

Property Condition

The physical state and general health of a real estate property, including all of its structures, systems, and components, is referred to as the property condition. To make educated decisions and sidestep pitfalls, it is essential to know the property's condition before buying or selling real estate. The outside and interior, as well as the building's mechanical systems, structural soundness, and safety measures, are all evaluated during a comprehensive property condition evaluation.

The state of a property is a major factor in determining its market value and desirability. A property that has been well-kept will likely sell faster and for more money. However, the market value and closing expenses may be affected by the need for repairs or improvements to bring a poorly maintained home up to par.

Professionals like home inspectors and licensed property assessors typically conduct these inspections. All readily accessible parts of the property are evaluated during these inspections.

Roof, siding, windows, doors, gutters, landscaping, and the driveway are all exterior characteristics that should be inspected. Damage, wear, and structural problems are recorded if present.

The walls, ceilings, flooring, doors, and windows on the inside are all inspected to determine how well they are holding up. Water damage, cracks, and other flaws that could reduce the property's livability or market value are among the things they inspect.

The state of the mechanical systems, such as the heating, ventilation, and air conditioning (HVAC), plumbing, electrical, water heater, and appliance systems, must be evaluated. The objective is to guarantee that these technologies work properly and are secure enough.

Foundation, walls, and other structural elements are inspected for signs of damage, settling, or instability as part of a thorough inspection of the property's structural integrity.

Smoke detectors, carbon monoxide detectors, fire extinguishers, and handrails are all examples of safety equipment that are accounted for and tested during property condition evaluations.

Mold, lead paint, radon, and asbestos are just some of the environmental risks that inspectors may look for.

Property Surveys

A property survey is an in-depth map or sketch that specifies the location, size, and other legal aspects of a certain parcel of land. Licensed surveyors conduct property surveys, which help define property borders, identify easements, and comprehend a property's physical layout. Dimensions, borders, and encroachment information are all provided by these surveys, so you know exactly what you're buying.

The following elements are generally included in property surveys:

Disputes between neighbors can be avoided by using a property survey to determine the exact boundaries of each property. Physical markers, such as stakes or pins, are used to demarcate boundary lines, which are then displayed on a survey map.

Access to utilities or the use of a common driveway are examples of the kinds of uses for which a property owner may offer a third party the right to utilize a piece of their land. Existing easements can be located and correctly recorded with the help of a survey.

Buildings, fences, and outbuildings are depicted on the survey map, along with any other improvements already present on the land. Planning and development of real estate can benefit greatly from this data.

Elevation changes and other topographical elements, such as bodies of water and hills, may be noted in a property's survey.

When a building or other object from one property extends into territory that belongs to another, this is known as an incursion. When property owners conduct surveys, they can learn about any possible encroachments and take action before the problem gets worse.

The legal descriptions in property surveys are used in property deeds and other legal documents.

Surveys are essential for anybody involved in the purchase or sale of real estate. To avoid any surprises, purchasers can check that they are getting the right bounds. Transparency is improved when sellers supply buyers with precise border details. Lenders also frequently necessitate property surveys before extending credit.

Required Property Disclosures

Sellers are obligated to disclose material facts about the property's condition, history, and any concerns to prospective buyers. These declarations are meant to be clear and give potential buyers all the data they need to make an informed choice. Legal requirements for sellers to disclose information that could influence a buyer's choice to purchase a property differ by country.

Property disclosure laws exist to safeguard purchasers from unwittingly purchasing homes with undetected flaws. By being up-front about these issues, sellers can head off potential conflicts and lawsuits from buyers who find hidden flaws after the sale.

The mandatory property disclosures include the following common areas:

Foundation concerns, roof leaks, and termite infestation are examples of structural defects that sellers must reveal to potential buyers.

Buyers should be made aware of the possible risks of mold and mildew by being told about any water damage, leaks, flooding history, or drainage problems.

Possible Environmental Dangers Property sellers may be required to declare the presence of any known or suspected environmental dangers, such as lead-based paint, asbestos, or buried storage tanks.

If there has been a history of mold or pest infestation on the property, the seller is obligated to disclose that fact.

Seller disclosures cover the HVAC, plumbing, electrical, and appliance systems in a home, as well as their general age and condition.

Recent Maintenance or Improvements: All recent maintenance or improvements to the property, including permits and contractor information, must be disclosed.

Problems with the Law and Zoning The sellers of a property may be required to reveal details regarding the property's zoning, land use limitations, and any pending legal challenges.

Sellers may be required to give information regarding potential noise or nuisances in the area, such as particularly loud neighbors, an airport, or adjacent construction.

While sellers are typically obligated to disclose relevant facts, the specifics of what must be disclosed might vary by jurisdiction and even property type. Buyers should read these disclosures thoroughly and may also opt to conduct their own inspections to double check the information.

Seller's Disclosure Obligations

In accordance with the law, sellers of real estate must disclose material facts regarding the property's physical condition and ownership history to prospective purchasers. Real estate laws and regulations in the jurisdiction where the property is located usually apply to these responsibilities.

To prevent buyers from purchasing houses with concealed faults or concerns, the law requires sellers to be forthright about those defects or issues. Sellers risk legal action, like litigation or contract termination, if they fail to meet these requirements.

Some of the most important things a merchant must tell you are:

Integrity: Sellers are obligated to disclose all material facts regarding the property's condition, history, and any concerns. All problems, obvious or not, that reduce the property's worth or make it uninhabitable are included here.

Proper timing: Disclosures are often made by sellers during the offer or contract negotiation phase of a deal. Potential purchasers can make better judgments when given accurate and timely information.

Disclosure Forms that Meet National Standards Many jurisdictions now compel merchants to use standardized disclosure forms. These documents contain various aspects of the property's history, current status, and any problems that have been identified.

Information that a reasonable buyer would find relevant in making a purchase choice is called "material facts," and sellers have an obligation to provide it. Details regarding structural problems, potential dangers to the environment, necessary repairs, and other topics may be included.

Disclosures may need to be revised if new information becomes available after they have been initially provided.

Sellers may not knowingly withhold material facts about the property or make false statements regarding its condition. If a seller knowingly conceals something from a buyer, they may face legal consequences.

While sellers must be forthright about any problems with the property, they need not conduct any inspections before to listing it for sale. However, many homeowners decide to have inspections done before putting their home on the market.

To guarantee compliance, sellers should consult with their real estate agent or legal counsel to learn about and understand the unique disclosure requirements in their jurisdiction. However, buyers should not rely solely on the seller's disclosures but rather conduct their own inspections to ensure the property is in satisfactory condition.

Impact of Disclosures on Property Transactions

Disclosures are extremely important components of the real estate transaction process since they supply buyers with valuable information regarding the property's condition, history, and potential problems. The impact of disclosures on real estate transactions is substantial, having an effect not only on the decision-making processes of purchasers but also on the legal requirements of vendors. The following are the ways in which disclosures affect real estate transactions:

Making Informed Decisions: Buyers depend on disclosures to help them make informed decisions about whether or not to move forward with a transaction. The information that is revealed assists buyers in determining the worth of the property, as well as the potential dangers involved and the amount of any necessary repairs or renovations. Disclosures provide prospective purchasers with the information they need to determine whether or not the property meets their individual tastes and criteria.

The information that is made public in the property disclosures might have an effect on the negotiations that take place between buyers and sellers. If there are known problems with the property, prospective purchasers may negotiate for repairs, price reductions, or other concessions based on the information that has been revealed. On the other hand, real estate that has been thoroughly disclosed and has a track record of success may garner greater offers.

Building confidence between buyers and sellers requires transparency, which can be achieved by providing disclosures that are accurate and comprehensive. Because it fosters a constructive atmosphere for negotiations and lowers the possibility of disagreements after the sale, sellers who are honest about the existence of potential issues are highly valued by purchasers.

Compliance with the law: The law requires sellers in many jurisdictions to comply with particular disclosure requirements when dealing with buyers. In the event that these conditions are not met, there may be legal repercussions, such as the termination of contracts, the filing of litigation, or the imposition of financial fines.

Reduced Liability: Proper disclosures can help lessen the potential of legal claims being filed against sellers by buyers who find previously hidden flaws or difficulties after a sale has taken place. When sellers are clean about any issues they are aware of up front, they reduce the likelihood that they will be accused of making false representations or engaging in fraudulent activity.

Accurate disclosures help make property transactions run more smoothly, which is beneficial to all parties involved. Both parties may move on with the transaction knowing that there will be no last-minute surprises or disagreements. Buyers can proceed with confidence, knowing that they have a full grasp of the property, while sellers can avoid either.

Concealment and Nondisclosure Risks

In the context of real estate transactions, concealment and nondisclosure are terms that relate to the purposeful act of hiding material information about a property or the failure to disclose that information. Both buyers and sellers are exposed to severe dangers when information is withheld or concealed when making transactions.

The viewpoint of the purchaser:

Unanticipated Expenses: Buyers who purchase houses with concealed flaws or difficulties may be subject to unforeseen expenses for repairs in the future. It's possible that they won't learn about these issues until after the transaction is complete, which could put a strain on their finances.

Reduced Marketability and Value Hidden flaws in a property might make it less desirable to potential buyers and lower its value. If there are problems with the property that have not been revealed, the new owners may have a difficult time reselling or renting it in the future.

Legal Action: Buyers who uncover undisclosed flaws in the product have the option of initiating legal action against the vendor on the grounds that the seller misrepresented the product or committed fraud. Legal proceedings can be emotionally stressful for all parties, in addition to being time-consuming and expensive.

A breach in confidence can occur when there is insufficient transparency between the parties involved (in this case, buyers and sellers). Potential purchasers may form unfavorable opinions of both the seller and the property if they believe they have been misled.

The viewpoint of the seller:

Legal Consequences Buyers have the right to take legal action against sellers who knowingly conceal or fail to disclose material flaws in their products. The filing of a lawsuit can result in monetary fines, damages, and additional fees related to the legal process.

Damage to Reputation: Sellers who are found guilty of hiding information run the risk of having their reputation harmed within the community of real estate professionals. Because of this, in the future, they might have a harder time selling homes, which would be bad for their professional status.

The buyer may have the legal right to void the contract and cancel the sale in certain circumstances, such as when significant flaws in the product are identified after it has already been purchased. Because of this, sellers could be put in an awkward position, where they are required to pay back the purchase price in addition to any other fees.

Legal Expenses Those sellers who are threatened with legal action because of their failure to disclose may be required to pay significant legal expenses in order to defend themselves in court.

Potential Legal Consequences of Inadequate Disclosures

In real estate transactions, failing to provide necessary disclosures can result in a variety of legal repercussions for both the purchasers and the sellers of the property. Legal action may be necessary if a violation of real estate law involves nondisclosure, misrepresentation, fraud, or another prohibited practice. The following is a list of possible legal consequences:

It is possible for a buyer to exercise their right to cancel a sale in the event that the buyer finds out after the sale about substantial flaws or problems that were not disclosed. This indicates that customers have the ability to call off the transaction and get a full refund of the money they spent.

Damages: Buyers have the right to seek damages if they can provide evidence that a seller willfully hid or misrepresented information. The term "damages" can refer to compensation for a variety of costs and losses, including those associated with the need for repairs, a drop in property value, and other monetary issues.

The buyer is required to show that they would not have entered the transaction if they had been aware of the undisclosed issues in order for the court to order the seller to satisfy the terms of the contract. This type of performance is known as specific performance.

Legal Fees In the event that conflicts emerge as a result of poor disclosures, both purchasers and sellers are at risk of incurring hefty legal fees. This covers the price of hiring an attorney, going to court, and any other expenditures associated with this matter.

Claims of Fraud: A seller may be subject to criminal and civil responsibility if a court finds that the seller willfully misrepresented information or participated in fraudulent behavior.

Loss of Earnest Money: Buyers who find undiscovered problems in the property and elect to back out of the purchase may be eligible to receive a refund of their earnest money deposit. However, this is not guaranteed.

Sellers who do not abide by the disclosure rules and regulations may be subject to regulatory penalties issued by the local real estate authorities if they do not comply with these laws and regulations.

It is essential for sellers to offer disclosures that are accurate and comprehensive, and it is as important for buyers to carefully evaluate these disclosures and conduct their own inspections, where necessary, in order to reduce the possibility of facing legal repercussions. Real estate specialists such as agents and attorneys can offer advise to both parties in a transaction to ensure compliance with disclosure laws and limit the likelihood of legal problems arising from the situation.

8.

Contract

Transactions involving real estate are based on solid ground thanks to the use of legally binding contracts. Contracts serve as the legally enforceable agreements that define the conditions, rights, and duties of all parties involved in the complex world of property transactions. Every player in a real estate transaction, from buyers and sellers to agents and attorneys, is touched in some way by the subtleties of the contracts that are involved.

In the context of real estate, this chapter explores the fundamental sphere of contracts and their implications. It presents an in-depth analysis of the fundamental ideas, guidelines, and factors that play a role in the formulation, performance, and termination of contracts in real estate transactions. The readers will get a thorough awareness of the role that contracts play in guaranteeing openness, fairness, and legal compliance throughout the entirety of the real estate transaction process by digging into the complexities of contracts.

A contract is more than just an agreement; it is an obligation that is legally binding and depends on certain stipulations being met. The principle that underlies all legitimate contracts is the concept of "mutual assent," which states that both parties must freely and voluntarily consent to the stipulations of the agreement. A simple promise can be transformed into a legally binding contract by including elements such as competent parties, consideration, and a lawful purpose. These elements are all necessary for a contract to exist.

Not every agreement is etched in stone; certain contracts can be invalid, voidable, or not enforceable at all. In the world of real estate, having a solid grasp of these distinctions is of the utmost importance. In contrast to void contracts, which never had any force of law to begin with, voidable contracts can be terminated if particular conditions are met. Contracts that are not enforceable cannot be enforced for either legal or procedural grounds, despite the fact that the contracts themselves are lawful. Participants in real estate transactions need to have a solid understanding of the ramifications of these classifications in order to navigate the landscape of contractual obligations with clarity and insight.

An offer is the first step on the path that leads from a casual discussion to a contract that is legally binding. An offer is an indication of intent to enter into an agreement under specified parameters. The transaction is considered finalized when an offer is met with an affirmative response known as acceptance. Nevertheless, in order for an agreement to be legally binding, it is necessary for both parties to exchange something of value in the form of consideration before the contract is finalized. These three elements—the offer, the acceptance, and the consideration—come together to form the essential connection that solidifies intentions into commitments.

There are many different kinds of real estate contracts, and each one is designed to cover a specific aspect of a different kind of property transaction. The environment is as diverse as the individual properties that are up for sale, encompassing anything from straightforward home purchase agreements to intricate commercial leasing contracts and option agreements. Being familiar with these different types of contracts gives both inexperienced buyers and sellers as well as seasoned experts the ability to navigate the complex landscape of real estate transactions.

Contracts for the purchase and sale of real estate, which are the backbone of all property transactions, are formed of many essential parts. These include the parties involved, the description of the property, the purchase price, any conditions that may apply, the amount of the earnest money deposit, and the date on which the transaction will be finalized. A participant's ability to effectively handle negotiations and live up to their duties depends on their level of mastery of the components listed above.

The traditional use of paper papers or the digital arena, in accordance with the Uniform Electronic Transactions Act (UETA), can both serve as the basis for the formation of contracts. In order to complete the process, there must be a manifest expression of intent and a mutual comprehension of the stipulations of the agreement. This is true regardless of the media used. Participants can confidently engage in transactions that represent their mutual understanding if the process of creation is demystified so that they know what to expect.

A crucial turning point in the process of purchasing real estate is when an offer is converted into a legally binding contract, more particularly a purchase agreement. This agreement summarizes the terms that were negotiated and holds both parties accountable for their respective responsibilities. When all parties involved have a clear understanding of this crucial turning point, they can move on with complete self-assurance.

Electronic signatures and communications have become widespread as a result of the digital age, ushering in a new era in the process of legally binding contract execution. The Uniform Electronic Transactions Act (UETA) legitimizes the use of electronic signatures and records in business transactions. This makes it possible for the digital world to have the same level of legal force as traditional contracts. This action not only makes things more convenient, but it also highlights the ever-changing character of the way contracts are carried out.

Multiple offers are not an uncommon occurrence in real estate markets that are characterized by high levels of competition. It is necessary to navigate this scenario with sensitivity in order to guarantee that all persons concerned are treated fairly. It is necessary for real estate professionals as well as individuals to have strategies for evaluating, negotiating, and selecting the offer that is most suited to their needs.

Addendums, amendments, and even specific contract terms can be used to modify a binding agreement so that it remains relevant even in the face of shifting conditions. These methods make it possible to make adjustments to meet ever-changing needs while still conforming to the standards of the law. Participants get the ability to ensure that their contracts continue to be accurate and current when they have a good understanding of these tools.

Real estate contracts typically include a number of contingencies, which allow for more flexibility and help mitigate risk. These requirements, which must be satisfied in order for the contract to move forward, include things like inspections, finance, and appraisals, among other things. In order for participants to be able to make decisions that are based on accurate information throughout the transaction, they need to understand the ramifications of various eventualities.

Contracts define the rights and obligations of the parties involved, so dictating the range of behaviors that are acceptable as well as the standards that must be met to fulfill promises. These rights include the ability to seek remedies in the event of a breach of the contract and the right to enforce the contract itself. On the other hand, the obligations involve transparency, correct disclosure, and prompt execution.

Despite the fact that contracts are designed to assure compliance, violations might nevertheless take place. When one of the parties to a contract does not live up to their commitments, this constitutes a breach of the contract. In these kinds of situations, the non-breaching party has a number of different options available to them for resolving the conflict, including the possibility of suing for damages, requesting particular performance, or canceling the contract altogether. Participants have more power to safeguard their interests and successfully handle breaches if they are aware of these remedies and how to use them.

Contracts reach their zenith at the phase known as execution, which is when all of the parties involved in the deal live up to their obligations and the deal is successfully finalized. Alternately, contracts may be cancelled for reasons such as mutual agreement between the parties or the occurrence of an event that no longer meets the criteria for the contingency. The successful completion of the voyage, which guarantees arrival at the targeted location and eases the passage into subsequent stages, is dependent on proper execution or termination.

In the context of real estate transactions, this chapter provides a complete breakdown of the convoluted world of contracts. Participants walk away with a comprehensive understanding of how contracts impact every stage of the real estate transaction, from the fundamental aspects of validity to the repercussions of breaches and the mechanics of termination. Individuals gain the ability to manage transactions with confidence, transparency, and legal savvy when they embrace this information and put it to use in their lives.

Elements of a Valid Contracts

A legally enforceable agreement between two or more parties that specifies the former's rights and the latter's responsibilities is known as a valid contract. In order for a contract to be valid, it needs to include a number of necessary components that guarantee its compliance with the law and its capacity to be carried out. Collectively, these components construct the framework within which parties can rely on the terms of the agreement and seek remedies in the event that the provisions are not satisfied.

An offer is a clear and explicit proposition made by one party (the offeror) to another (the offeree), expressing the purpose to enter into a contract with another party (the offeree) under specified terms. An offer is followed by an acceptance, which acknowledges that the terms of the offer are acceptable. The offeree's unequivocal consent to the terms of the offer is referred to as acceptance of the offer. Both the offer and the acceptance serve as evidence of the parties' mutual assent, which is an essential component in the process of making a contract.

The parties to a contract are required to provide one another with "consideration," which is defined as "something of value exchanged." It may take the shape of monetary compensation, the provision of goods or services, or even a commitment to carry out or abstain from a certain action. The exchange of consideration guarantees that both parties have something at stake in the contract and helps to avoid making promises for no reason.

The goal of the contract must be legitimate and cannot be in conflict with any existing laws or policies of the government. Illegitimate conduct that result in the formation of a contract, such as illicit gambling or fraud, are null and void and cannot be enforced.

Capacity It is imperative that all parties to the contract have the requisite authority under the law to enter into the agreement. This means that they need to be of legal age and mentally capable in order to comprehend the terms of the contract as well as the penalties of breaking it. People who are underage, under the influence of alcohol, or otherwise unable to make sound decisions may not have the legal competence to enter valid contracts.

In order for there to be mutual assent, also referred to as a "meeting of the minds," it is necessary for both parties to comprehend and concur with the fundamental stipulations of the contract. In the event that the terms are misunderstood or an error is made, the contract has the potential to be null and invalid or to be voidable.

Agreement That Is Made Freely The agreement to engage into the contract must be made free of any coercion, duress, undue influence, or fraudulent misrepresentation if it is to be considered voluntary. Any one of these situations could render a previously agreed upon contract null and void.

It is essential to keep in mind that the lack of any one of these components may render a contract null and void or unable to be carried out. In order to create a genuine and legally enforceable agreement, the parties involved need to make certain that all of the necessary components are included and are defined precisely.

Void, Voidable, and Unenforceable Contracts

It is vital to have an understanding of the classes of contracts, which include void, voidable, and unenforceable, in order to evaluate the legal standing of the contracts:

Contracts That Have No Legal Effect A contract that has no legal effect from the beginning is known as being void. It suffers from fundamental flaws as a result of variables such as the presence of unlawful subject matter or inadequate capacity. A void contract does not impose any legal responsibilities on the parties to it, and the law treats the agreement as though it never existed.

Contracts That Can Be Voided Although a voidable contract begins as being lawfully binding and enforceable, if certain conditions are met, one of the parties may exercise their right to void (cancel) the contract. Fraud, misrepresentation, improper influence, or an inability to handle the responsibility may all fall under this category. The party that has the ability to invalidate the contract has the choice of either continuing with the agreement or getting out of it.

Contracts That Are Not Able To Be Enforced In Court A contract that is not able to be enforced in court is considered to be valid despite the fact that it cannot be enforced in court for either technical or legal reasons. For instance, if a contract is not written down in accordance with the requirements of the Statute of Frauds, then the contract may not be enforceable. In spite of the fact that the parties may have agreed to the agreements, they are not permitted to pursue legal remedies through the courts.

Offer, Acceptance, and Consideration

The fundamental ideas that form the basis of a contract are known as the "offer," "acceptance," and "consideration," respectively.

An offer is a clear, definite, and unconditional proposal that is made by one party (the offeror) to another (the offeree) with the goal of making a binding agreement with the offeree in the event that the offeree accepts the conditions as they are provided.

Acceptance: Acceptance is when the person who has been offered something gives a positive reaction to the conditions of the offer. For there to be a legitimate contract, it is necessary that the conditions of the contract be disclosed to the person who made the offer. In most cases, maintaining silence does not indicate endorsement of something.

The term "consideration" refers to the monetary or other form of legal value that is exchanged between the parties. It could be monetary value, the provision of products or services, or even a promise. The exchange of consideration guarantees that both parties are delivering something of value in exchange for the commitments they have made. A reciprocal obligation, which is required for a contract to be enforceable, cannot exist if there is no consideration exchanged.

These ideas are essential to the process of putting together a contract. When a party makes an offer that is accepted in exchange for anything of value, they have laid the groundwork for the formation of a legally enforceable agreement.

Contract Types in Real Estate

Real estate transactions require a number of different forms of contracts, each of which is customized to a certain set of circumstances:

Purchase Agreement: Also referred to as a sales contract, this is the most important contract in the process of buying or selling real estate. It details the terms of the sale, including the purchase price, any conditions that must be met, the closing date, and any other pertinent information.

Lease Agreement: A lease agreement is a contract between a landlord and a tenant that outlines the conditions under which the tenant will rent a property from the landlord. It provides information regarding the rent, the length of the lease, the responsibilities, and the restrictions.

Option Agreement: An option agreement offers a party the right, but not the responsibility, to buy or sell a property at a predetermined price within a specified time frame. This right is granted in exchange for the payment of a predetermined option fee.

Listing Agreement: This agreement is between a property owner and a real estate agent, and it outlines the terms under which the agent will market and sell the property. The agreement is between the owner of the property and the real estate agent.

Land Contract: A land contract, also known as a contract for deed or an installment sale agreement, enables a buyer to make payments directly to the seller over time while dwelling on the property. Other names for a land contract include contract for deed and installment sale agreement. When all of the payments have been made, ownership will change hands.

A contract known as an assignment contract is one that transfers the rights and responsibilities of one party's involvement in a contract to the involvement of another party. When an investor sells their option to buy a property to another buyer, this is one of the common outcomes.

In the area of real estate transactions, each of these types of contracts has a unique purpose, which enables the parties to traverse a variety of eventualities with clarity and legal certainty.

Common Components of a Real Estate Sales Contracts

The most important document that establishes the conditions of a property transaction between a buyer and a seller is a real estate sales contract, which is also known as a purchase agreement. This document is also known as a purchase agreement. This contract serves as the road map that directs the path from the acceptance of the offer to the completion of the transaction. It describes the rights, obligations, and expectations of both parties. The following is a list of the typical components included in a sales contract for real estate:

Parties to the Contract: At the very beginning of the agreement, both the buyer and the seller are named as the parties to the contract. Their proper names, residences, and other contact information are presented in a clear and concise manner.

Description of the Property: Presented below is a comprehensive and correct description of the property that is up for sale. This contains the property's street address, its legal description (which is derived from surveys and property records), and any other pertinent information regarding the property's borders, lot size, and improvements.

Purchase Price The purchase price that has been agreed upon for the piece of property is outlined in the contract. This can include the entire price, any down payment or earnest money deposit, and the method of payment for the remaining balance of the purchase price.

Earnest Money Deposit: This is a deposit made by the buyer in good faith to establish their sincere intent to purchase the property. Earnest money deposits are also known as good faith deposits. The contract provides specific information regarding the amount, the terms under which the deposit may be refunded or lost, and the deadline for making the deposit.

The term "contingencies" refers to the conditions that need to be fulfilled in order for the contract to move forward. The sale of the buyer's current home, financing, an examination of the target property, and an appraisal are all examples of common conditions. The contract details the timelines and processes that must be followed in order to satisfy these unforeseen circumstances.

Date of Closing: The closing date is a date that is determined by the contract, and it is the day that the property is formally transferred from the seller to the buyer. This date is very important since it defines when the buyer takes possession of the property and when ownership of the property changes hands.

Title and Deed: The contract discusses the current state of the property's title as well as the kind of deed that will be used for the transfer of ownership of the property. Additionally, it may define who is accountable for acquiring title insurance and doing a title search on the property.

Property Condition: The contract might include clauses related to the property's condition, detailing whether the property will be sold "as is" or with particular repairs and upgrades completed by the seller before the closing date and time is reached.

Transfer Taxes, Title Insurance Fees, and Attorney Fees are some of the Closing charges that are outlined in the Contract. The contract also specifies which party is responsible for paying these charges. There is room for negotiation between the buyer and the seller on these costs.

Default and Remedies: This section outlines the repercussions that will occur in the event that either party does not fulfill their commitments as outlined in the contract. It describes the options open to the non-defaulting party, such as keeping the earnest money deposit or taking legal action if the other party defaults on their obligations.

Brokerage Fees In the event that real estate agents are involved in the transaction, the contract will outline the commissions that are expected to be paid to both the buyer's and the seller's agents.

Signatures: The contract cannot be considered legitimate unless all of the parties concerned have signed it. The exchange of signatures indicates that both parties have accepted all of the terms and conditions contained in the contract.

How Contracts are Created

In the realm of real estate, the formation of contracts can take place via a variety of methods, each of which requires a showing of intent, agreement, and communication:

The purchaser will normally initiate the process by submitting an offer to purchase the property. The offer details the intended purchase price, as well as any applicable conditions and other clauses. The terms that have been presented make it clear that the party making the offer intends to enter into a contract.

Acceptance: Once the seller has received the offer, they have the option to either accept it, reject it, or make a counteroffer. When a seller agrees to the terms of an offer without making any modifications, the transaction is considered accepted. It is absolutely necessary that the terms of the original offer are reflected in the acceptance in order to establish a binding agreement between both parties.

Communication: In order for a contract to be enforceable, it is necessary for the parties to have open and honest dialogue with one another. Depending on the laws of the applicable jurisdiction and the stipulations of the agreement, this may take the shape of either written or spoken communication.

Consideration: The idea of consideration, which refers to the trading of something of value for another of equal or greater worth, comes into play here. The promise to buy a piece of property in exchange for monetary payment is a common form of consideration in real estate transactions.

"Meeting of the Minds": The "meeting of the minds" is a vital component in the process of contract formation. This refers to the point at when both parties have an understanding of and are in agreement regarding the fundamental terms of the contract. This ensures that there is agreement between both parties and that there are no misunderstandings.

When an Offer Becomes a Contract (Purchase Agreement)

When an offer is converted into a purchase agreement, the transaction is considered to have reached a critical juncture and the deal is considered to be finalized. This change requires numerous important processes, including:

The buyer makes an offer to purchase the property, specifying the terms and circumstances of the transaction, and the seller must accept or reject the offer. If the seller accepts the terms as they are presented without making any changes, then the acceptance will serve as the basis for the purchase agreement.

Assent from Both Parties: In order to establish that both parties have "meeting of the minds" respecting the agreements, both parties must demonstrate mutual assent. To reach a point when both parties are satisfied with the transaction, it is necessary for the buyer's offer and the seller's acceptance to be in perfect alignment.

Consideration: The buyer's assurance that they will pay the purchase price, in addition to the earnest money deposit that they will offer, serves as consideration, which is a fundamental component of a valid contract.

Legal Formalities It is possible that the purchase agreement may be required to comply with certain legal formalities, such as being written down and signed by both parties. This requirement, however, will vary from jurisdiction to jurisdiction.

There is a possibility that the purchase agreement will contain contingencies, which are clauses that spell out various requirements that need to be satisfied before the contract can be finalized. These may include things like getting finance or passing inspections, among other considerations.

As soon as each of these components is in place, the offer is converted into a legally binding purchase agreement, which acts as the linchpin document for the duration of the transaction.

Uniform Electronic Transactions Act (UETA)

The ways in which legal agreements are drafted carried out, and conveyed have all been profoundly altered by the advent of the digital age. The Uniform Electronic Transactions Act, sometimes known as UETA, is a piece of legislation that provides a legal framework for ensuring that electronic contracts and signatures are valid and enforceable. The following is an explanation of how the UETA influences the development of contracts:

Legal Recognition: The UETA offers electronic documents and signatures the same legal status as their paper equivalents, guaranteeing that electronic contracts are just as legally valid as traditional ones. This is accomplished through the legal recognition of electronic records and signatures.

Both Parties Must Have Consented to Conduct Transactions Electronically In order for the UETA to be applicable, both parties must have consented to the conduct of transactions electronically. This can be accomplished either with the parties' explicit cooperation or over the course of their dealings with one another.

Authentication The UETA mandates that all electronic signatures be correctly attributed to their signatory. This guarantees that all parties engaged are responsible for upholding their commitments with one another.

Record Retention The UETA requires that electronic records be stored in a manner that allows for easy access, ensures their accuracy, and enables them to be reproduced for future reference.

The UETA has a broad scope and can be applied to a variety of different sorts of transactions, including real estate contracts. However, it's possible that certain kinds of documents, such wills and other paperwork related to family law, won't be included.

The provisions of the UETA have simplified the process of creating and executing contracts, making it possible for parties to engage in transactions in a manner that is more time and cost effective while preserving their legal standing. It has led the way for the use of electronic signatures, emails, and online platforms in the real estate market, which has resulted in transactions being completed more quickly, more easily, and with an increased level of safety.

Dealing with Multiple Offers

It is not at all unusual for a seller in a real estate market that is saturated with competition to receive more than one offer on their home. Both buyers and sellers might benefit from the chances and difficulties presented by the current circumstances. To successfully navigate several offers, you need to take a deliberate approach to ensure that the process is fair and transparent for all of the parties involved.

From the standpoint of the buyer, the prospect of competing with other offers can be intimidating. The following is a guide for buyers to help them manage this scenario:

It is imperative that you move quickly because time is of the utmost in a market that is very competitive. When a buyer discovers a home that they are interested in purchasing, they should move quickly in order to submit their offer before any other possible purchasers.

Strong first Bid: Ensure that your first bid is comparable to other bids. In a circumstance where there are several bids, it's possible that lowball offers won't be considered seriously. When determining how much of an offer to make, it is best to discuss the matter with your real estate agent.

Think About the Terms Although pricing is the most important factor, other terms might also influence a seller's selection. You can make your offer more tempting by being flexible with the closing dates, removing certain stipulations, or offering a bigger amount of earnest money as a deposit.

Personal Letter Composing a warm and sincere letter to the seller is one way to assist humanize your offer and show that you care about the transaction. It's possible that the seller will be moved by your narrative and the reasons you want the property if you share them.

From the seller's perspective, managing several offers necessitates doing an in-depth analysis of the following aspects of each offer:

It is important to communicate with your real estate agent about your objectives and priorities in order to set clear expectations. Are you interested in the best possible price, the quickest possible closing, or specified terms?

Examine Every Offer: In this step, you will examine every offer in great detail, taking into consideration the offer price, any conditions, financing options, and the qualifications of the purchasers.

You have the option to make a counteroffer to one or more purchasers in order to improve the terms of the bids that they have made. A competitive bidding process may result as a result of this.

Accepting an Offer Once you have made the decision to accept an offer, you should immediately notify the buyer who will be purchasing the property and their agent. To prevent misunderstandings, it is important to ensure that all parties are informed of the offer that has been accepted.

Ethical Considerations Both sellers and their agents have a responsibility to manage multiple offers in an ethical manner, ensuring that the process is both transparent and fair.

Addendums, Amendments, and Contract Clauses

The buying and selling of real estate may be a complicated process, and contracts frequently need to be modified to account for shifting conditions. Addendums, amendments, and contract clauses are all examples of methods that can be used to change or clarify terms of existing contracts without necessitating a full renegotiation of the terms.

Addendums: An addendum is a distinct document that is appended to the original contract in order to offer extra terms, conditions, or agreements. Addendums are also known as supplemental terms and conditions. Addendums that pertain to inspections, repairs, or shifts in closing dates are examples of frequently used addendums.

The term "amendment" refers to a modification that is made in a formal manner to the initial contract. It is necessary for there to be consensus among all of the parties concerned. It is possible to change anything in the contract through the use of amendments, including the purchase price, the conditions, or the closing date.

Contract clauses are predetermined terms and conditions that address certain eventualities and are included in contracts. The terms "appraisal contingencies," "financing contingencies," and "inspection contingencies" are all examples of common clauses. These clauses outline the necessary steps to follow in the event that a number of predetermined conditions are not satisfied.

Contingencies and Conditions

A real estate contract may contain a number of clauses known as contingencies and conditions. These provisions define particular requirements that must be satisfied before the deal can be executed. They safeguard both the buyer and the seller by enabling the possible problems to be resolved prior to the transaction's completion, which is when the transaction is considered to have been completed.

The contract is subject to cancellation if the buyer is unable to get financing to complete the acquisition of the property as outlined in the financing contingency clause. In the event that the purchaser is unable to get financing, the contract may be terminated without incurring any fees.

Inspection Contingency: The buyer is given the opportunity to have the property inspected by a qualified individual thanks to this contingency. In the event that substantial problems are found, the buyer has the option of either negotiating repairs or requesting a price reduction.

Appraisal Contingency: If the appraised value of the property is less than the purchase price, the buyer has the option to either renegotiate the price or back out of the contract under the terms of this contingency.

Sale Contingency: This contingency allows the buyer additional time to sell their present property before moving forward with the purchase of a new one in the event that the buyer needs to sell their current property in order to purchase a new one.

Rights and Obligations of Parties to a Contract

A real estate contract lays out the rights and responsibilities of all parties involved, including buyers, sellers, and even real estate agents in some instances. It is essential to have a thorough understanding of these rights and obligations in order to guarantee a transaction that is fair and goes off without a hitch.

Rights and Responsibilities of the Buyer:

Buyers have the legal right to inspect the property prior to closing and to make any requests for concessions or repairs depending on the results of the inspection.

Buyers have the responsibility of making all reasonable attempts to get financing and supplying the relevant papers to the lender in order to fulfill their financing obligations.

Earnest Money Deposit: In order to demonstrate their dedication to the transaction, buyers are required to give the earnest money deposit that was previously agreed upon.

Buyers are responsible for satisfying any and all contingencies mentioned in the purchase agreement. This includes securing financing and carrying out inspections as outlined in the document.

The Rights and Obligations of the Seller:

Sellers have the right to accept, reject, or counter any offers that are made to them. In addition, buyers have the right to accept, reject, or counter any offers that are made to them.

Property Disclosure: Sellers have a responsibility to give information that is both accurate and full regarding the condition of the property.

The seller is responsible for ensuring that the property has a clean title and assisting the buyer in taking ownership of the property.

Property Condition: Sellers are expected to deliver the property in the condition indicated in the contract, which may include performing repairs if they have been agreed upon by both parties.

Breach of Contract and Remedies

When one of the parties to a legally binding agreement does not fulfill their responsibilities in accordance with the terms of the agreement, this is considered a breach of contract. This failure may involve a failure to carry out a particular task, a failure to reach a deadline, or a failure to comply to any other terms that were agreed upon in the contract. There is a spectrum of severity associated with breaches, all of which can result in serious financial and legal repercussions for the entity that is at fault. The ability to resolve disagreements and maintain the validity of agreements requires a fundamental understanding of contract breach as well as the various potential remedies.

Variations of a Breach:

There are a few different categories of security holes that can be exploited:

A material breach of the contract occurs when there is a violation of the terms that is both major and serious and that gets to the core of the agreement. In most cases, it releases the party that did not break their responsibilities and can lead to legal action for damages.

A minor breach of the contract is when one party fails to fulfill a relatively minor obligation stipulated in the contract. This type of breach is sometimes referred to as a partial breach. It is still possible for the non-breaching party to pursue damages, but in the meantime, they must continue to fulfill their own commitments.

The term "anticipatory breach" refers to the situation that arises when one party discloses to the other that they will not perform their responsibilities in accordance with the terms of the agreement. Because of this, the non-breaching party may feel compelled to pursue legal action or take other measures deemed suitable.

Consequences of Violating:

When one party breaches a contract with another, the non-breaching party has numerous options on how to proceed, including the following:

Damages are typically awarded as the most prevalent kind of compensation when a contract has been broken. Damages are intended to reimburse the party who did not break the agreement for any financial losses that were sustained as a result of the breach. There are several distinct categories of damages, the most common of which are compensatory, consequential, and punitive damages.

Specific Performance: The court may impose specific performance in circumstances where monetary compensation is unable to adequately cure the violation. This indicates that the party that breached the contract is responsible for carrying out their duties as stipulated in the agreement.

The act of rescinding a contract means that the agreement in question is null and void, and that the parties are placed back in the positions they held before the formation of the contract. In most cases, this is utilized when the violation is serious to the point where it renders the contract null and void.

Returning any benefits obtained from the infringing party is one component of the legal concept known as "restitution." This is done in the interest of preventing unfair enrichment.

Reformation: If the provisions of the contract are not obvious or are confusing, the court may reform or amend the contract so that it more truly reflects the parties' initial purpose.

Execution or Termination

The two possible outcomes of a contract are execution and termination. These outcomes are determined by whether or not the parties to the contract fulfill their responsibilities, or whether the contract is terminated before its full term.

Carrying Out:

When a contract is "executed," it indicates that all of the parties involved have complied with their duties in accordance with the terms of the agreement. The transaction went exactly as planned, and all of the requirements outlined in the contract have been satisfied. The successful transfer of ownership from the seller to the buyer is often what is meant when referring to execution in the context of real estate transactions. This entails both the exchange of the purchase money and the transfer of the property title.

The end has come:

When either party to a contract decides to end it before the end of the contract's initial term or before the completion of the obligations that were agreed upon, the contract is said to have been terminated. There are many different scenarios that might lead to a relationship coming to an end, such as the parties involved coming to an agreement, a predetermined event taking place, or a violation of the terms of the contract.

Clauses for Early Termination:

Contracts typically include termination clauses that detail the conditions that must be met in order for the agreement to be scrapped and renegotiated. These provisions detail the processes and requirements that must be met in order to terminate the contract, including any notice requirements or fines that may apply.

The following are effects of terminating:

When a contract is terminated, all obligations imposed by the contract on either party are immediately null and void. Nevertheless, there is a possibility that the parties will not be released from any responsibilities or duties that have already incurred prior to the termination of the agreement.

9.

Leasing

•————————————•

The real estate market is built on leasing, which comprises a wide variety of agreements that make the temporary possession and use of properties easier. Leasing is an essential component of the sector. Leasing provides options for individuals, families, and organizations to inhabit and utilize real estate spaces without the long-term responsibilities that are associated with ownership of property. This dynamic alternative to property ownership can be applied to residential or commercial settings and offers a number of advantages over property ownership. This chapter goes deeper into the complicated realm of leasing, elucidating its knotty underpinnings and shining light on the essential facets that landlords and tenants alike are required to traverse successfully.

The development of lease agreements, which are legal papers that outline the terms, conditions, and duties of both parties—the landlord and the tenant—is the cornerstone of the leasing process. Residential lease agreements are tailored to meet the requirements of housing, whereas commercial lease agreements are tailored to meet the requirements of business or other non-residential uses. These agreements specify vital information such as the amount of rent, the payment schedule, the amount of the security deposit, the length of the lease, who is responsible for maintenance, and provisions for any potential disputes.

The length of time that a property is leased for is established by the terms of the lease. They can be extremely diverse, ranging from one-month leases to multi-year commitments and everything in between. At the time of a lease renewal, both parties have the opportunity to reassess the terms of the current lease agreement and determine whether or not to continue to be bound by it. During the process of renewing a lease, parties may engage in negotiations on adjustments to the monthly rent, term extensions, or clause modifications in the original agreement.

The sale of a leased property brings with it a host of complications that must be navigated with extreme caution. When the owner of a property that is rented out changes, there are repercussions for both the landlord and the renter in terms of their rights and responsibilities. It is possible that lease agreements may remain unchanged or will be revised, depending on the applicable legal restrictions and the consensus of all parties involved.

This chapter digs into the rights and responsibilities of both landlords and tenants, laying the groundwork for a happy relationship between the parties involved in the leasing arrangement. It is the responsibility of the landlord to ensure that the property is habitable at all times, attend to any necessary repairs, and uphold the terms of the lease. Tenants are expected not just to pay rent but also to comply to the property's use guidelines and keep the premises in a condition that is fair.

The unfavorable situation of being kicked out of one's home is investigated in further depth. Evictions can occur for a variety of reasons, including the tenant's failure to pay the required rent, a violation of the conditions of the lease, or the lease agreement's expiration. This chapter examines a variety of eviction processes, ranging from unlawful detainer actions to constructive evictions, and focuses on the legal steps that landlords need to take in order to reclaim ownership of their property.

Lease agreements all contain the same key components that are essential to their structure and capacity to be enforced. These features include information about the parties involved, a description of the property, the length of the lease, specifics about the rent, information about maintenance and repair responsibilities, as well as clauses that address dispute resolution and termination.

The chapter comes to a close by delivering some important information regarding the procedures of collecting rent and evicting tenants. Clear methods, several payment choices, and compliance with all applicable legal restrictions are necessary for effective rent collecting. In the event that a dispute or a tenant's failure to comply with the terms of the lease arises, landlords are required to be familiar with the eviction procedures outlined in the applicable local legislation in order to guarantee a legitimate and just procedure.

This chapter provides readers with an in-depth understanding of the complexities associated with residential and commercial lease agreements, the rights and responsibilities of both landlords and tenants, the complexities of lease renewals, the complexities surrounding property sales within lease arrangements, and the unfortunate but necessary procedures for eviction and rent collection. This helps readers navigate the multifaceted realm of leasing. The parties involved in leasing agreements are able to make educated judgments, cultivate positive relationships, and successfully traverse the dynamic landscape of property occupation and use when armed with this comprehensive knowledge.

Residential and Commercial Lease Agreements

Residential Lease Agreements:

Lease Agreements for Residential Property A lease agreement for a residential property is a legal contract between a landlord and a tenant that outlines the terms and conditions under which a residential property is rented. Residential lease agreements are often used in the United States. These agreements serve as the basis for the landlord-tenant relationship, laying out the rights and responsibilities of each side and serving as the foundation for the partnership. Leases for residential properties include contracts for apartments, houses, condominiums, and townhouses, amongst other forms of living accommodations. The following are some of the most important aspects of a residential lease agreement:

Parties and Property Information: The agreement specifies both the landlord and the tenant, as well as their respective contact information. Additionally, the agreement provides details regarding the property. Additionally, it contains an in-depth description of the real estate that is being rented, along with the property's address and any particular features.

The length of time that the property is rented for is denoted by the "lease term," which can be found in the rental agreement. There is a wide range of possible lease periods, from month-to-month agreements to leases that last a year or longer.

The agreement specifies not only the monthly rent amount but also the manner in which it is to be paid as well as the frequency of such payments. It is also possible for it to indicate late fees for rent that is paid late.

A security deposit is something that is required to be paid by renters under the terms of many residential lease agreements. This deposit will serve as protection for the landlord in the event that the property is damaged or the rent is not paid on time. The agreement specifies both the total amount of the deposit and the terms under which it will be refunded.

Repairs and Maintenance: The maintenance and repair responsibilities are laid out in explicit detail in the agreement. It lays forth which party is accountable for particular responsibilities, such as mowing the yard, making repairs, and maintaining the appliances.

Use and Occupancy: The lease agreement outlines the permitted uses for the property as well as the people who are allowed to live there. Concerns relating to pets, subletting, and other aspects of occupation are discussed in this section.

Both the procedures for cancelling the lease and the choices for renewing it are outlined in great detail. Included below are the required notice periods for terminating the lease as well as the procedures to follow in order to prolong the term of the lease.

Commercial Lease Agreements:

The leasing of properties for commercial or other non-residential purposes is governed by the agreements known as commercial leases. These leases are more difficult to understand than residential leases since commercial renters have a wider variety of needs and commercial tenants run a wider variety of enterprises, each of which has its own set of specialized criteria. Lease agreements for commercial properties can look very different depending on a number of aspects, including the building type (retail, office, or industrial), the lease periods, and the nature of the business. The following are some of the most important aspects of a business leasing agreement:

There are three different types of leases that can be used for commercial properties: gross leases, net leases, and modified gross leases. Each type outlines the specifics of how the rent and other expenses are computed, as well as who is responsible for what portion of those costs.

The rent structure describes the base rent amount as well as any other charges that may apply, such as property taxes, insurance, or maintenance fees. Rent increases over the term of a commercial lease are a topic that frequently needs to be negotiated.

Use section: The use that the tenant is permitted to make of the rented space is outlined in this section. It is possible for there to be limitations placed on particular activities or categories of businesses in order to preserve a pleasant environment for all of the tenants.

renovations Made by the Tenant Many commercial lease agreements give tenants the right to make renovations or alterations to the space in order to better accommodate their operations. The extent of allowed upgrades as well as who is accountable for the expense of such improvements are both outlined in the agreement.

The length of time a commercial lease is in effect can be quite substantial, typically running for a number of years. The lease duration, as well as any options for renewal and any rent increases that may apply during renewal periods, are all spelled out in the agreement.

Assignment and Subletting: This provision defines if the tenant is authorized to assign the lease to another party or sublet the space to a third party. It also specifies whether the tenant is allowed to sublet the space to a third party.

Maintenance and Repairs: The tenant's responsibilities for the property's maintenance and repairs are outlined, and this may include any requirements that the tenant return the space to its former condition at the conclusion of the lease.

Lease Terms and Renewals

The length of time that the tenant is responsible for paying rent on the leased property is referred to as the lease term. The terms of a lease are subject to extensive variation depending on the type of property, the preferences of the parties, and the conditions of the local market. The period of a residential lease often ranges from six months to one year, whereas the term of a business lease might extend several years, typically anywhere from five to 10 years or even longer. The length of time during which the tenant is permitted to occupy the premises and the landlord is entitled to financial compensation in the form of rent is referred to as the lease term, and it is outlined in the tenancy agreement.

Lease Renewals: Lease renewals take place when the initial period of the lease is getting close to its end and both parties negotiate whether or not to extend the lease for another term. During lease renewal negotiations, prospective alterations to the lease terms, such as increases or decreases in rent, length of the lease, and any other modifications, are on the table for discussion. Both the renter and the landlord stand to benefit from renewal options: tenants may keep their occupancy and stability, while landlords can avoid the possibility of vacancy. It is essential for the landlord and the tenant to have a conversation well in advance of the lease's expiration date in order to go through the renewal terms and make preparations for a seamless transition in the event that a renewal is agreed upon.

Sale of a Leased Property (Transfer of Ownership)

When selling a property that is being rented out, there are a number of special factors to consider that can have an effect not just on the landlord but also on the renter. The terms and duties of a lease agreement do not immediately become null and void in the event that a property is sold. Instead, the new owner of the property is normally responsible for transferring the lease agreement to the tenant, which ensures that the tenant's rights and obligations are not affected. The following are the most important considerations to make:

Rights and Obligations: The lease agreement does not change in any way regardless of whether or not the leased property is sold. This includes the tenant's rights and obligations. The new owner takes over the role of landlord from the former owner and assumes their responsibilities.

Notification: In some jurisdictions, renters may have the legal right to be notified of the impending sale of the property. Because of this, they are able to be informed about the change in ownership as well as the contact information for the new landlord.

Deposits of Security: In most cases, the new owner will be responsible for the transfer of the security deposit from the prior owner. The tenant retains all of their rights with regard to the security deposit.

Terms of the Lease The terms of the lease, including the rent, the duration of the lease, and any other terms, will not alter unless both parties agree to the modifications.

Provisions of the Lease It is essential for the buyer and the seller to go over the lease agreement during the process of selling the property in order to gain an understanding of the lease's terms and obligations.

Buyers of leased properties have an obligation to perform their own due diligence, which includes reading over any existing lease agreements and gaining an understanding of the present tenants' rights and duties.

Consent from Tenants: Certain lease agreements may contain terms that require tenant consent before the property may be sold to a new owner. In these kinds of circumstances, the agreement of the tenant might be required before the sale can go through.

When selling a home that is being rented out, it is important for all parties involved—the seller, the buyer, and the tenant—to have open lines of communication and work together to meet all of their respective legal responsibilities.

Landlord and Tenant Rights and Obligations

There is a set of rights and responsibilities that govern the landlord-tenant relationship and guarantee a legal and equitable lease. In order to successfully negotiate the leasing process and maintain a peaceful living or working environment, it is essential for both parties to have a thorough understanding of these rights and obligations.

Landlord's Rights and Obligations:

Landlords have the legal authority to collect rent from Tenants in line with the terms and conditions of the Lease.

Landlords have the right to enter the premises for maintenance, repairs, inspections, and emergency situations. However, they must give appropriate warning in accordance with applicable legislation.

Landlords have a responsibility to ensure that their properties are suitable for human habitation at all times. This includes ensuring the reliability of utilities like water, heat, and power.

Landlords must make all necessary repairs and upkeep to the property in order to keep it in habitable condition. Claims for breach of contract may result from ignoring the need for repairs.

Landlords have the option of requiring a security deposit from their tenants as protection against tenant damage to property or rent nonpayment. All security deposits will be handled in accordance with applicable laws.

Landlords are obligated to advise tenants of certain matters, including the presence of lead-based paint (if any) and the state of the rental unit.

Nondiscrimination: Landlords must abide by fair housing rules that forbid bias based on a person's race, religion, gender, sexual orientation, disability, or other protected characteristic.

Tenant's Rights and Obligations:

Tenants are entitled to the peaceful use of the rental unit without disturbance from the Landlord. Owners of rental properties are not allowed unannounced or without a good reason.

Tenants must pay rent in accordance with the lease's terms. Eviction is possible if rent is late.

Tenants are responsible for keeping the rental unit in a habitable condition and for preventing any damage to the property beyond what is considered to be normal wear and tear.

Tenants are responsible for following all lease provisions, including any and all laws and regulations.

If a security deposit is needed, the tenant is responsible for providing one and has the right to receive it back at the lease's conclusion, less any reasonable deductions.

Landlords are required to treat tenants equally and fairly regardless of any legally protected traits.

Types of Eviction

When a tenant is evicted, the landlord is able to lawfully reclaim ownership of the rented unit. There are many different types of evictions that must adhere to different legal protocols. Types of evictions that are common include:

The most prevalent cause of eviction is arrears in rent payments. After giving the required amount of notice, a landlord can begin eviction procedures if a tenant has not paid rent.

Eviction proceedings can be initiated by the landlord if the tenant breaches the lease agreement by, for example, conducting illegal activities on the premises.

If the lease term has ended and the tenant has not vacated the premises or renewed the lease, the landlord may begin the eviction process.

Tenant eviction for nuisance or damage occurs when a tenant causes significant distress to other tenants or to the property itself.

Tenant can be evicted if the landlord discovers illegal activity taking place on the premises.

Landlords can legally evict tenants in some areas if they plan to move into the rental unit themselves or have a member of their immediate family do so.

Common Elements of a Lease Agreement

Leasing relationships have a defined structure thanks to the main aspects included in lease agreements. These features make certain that each party knows what is expected of them. Elements shared between them are:

A description of the premises and the parties involved are included in this section of the lease. A thorough description of the rented property is also included.

Whether the lease is month-to-month, for a certain period of time, or for a longer period of time is set forth in the agreement. It also specifies what needs to be done when a lease expires.

The amount of rent due, when it's due, and what kinds of payments are acceptable are all spelled out in the agreement.

If a security deposit is required, the terms under which it will be returned are specified in the agreement.

Repairs and Upkeep: The agreement spells out who is liable for what in terms of repairs and upkeep.

This section specifies the permitted uses of the property and the people who are allowed to live there. There could be rules about subletting, pets, and other issues.

Procedures for early lease termination and required notice periods are spelled forth in the lease's termination clause.

Rent Collection and Eviction Procedures

Rent Collection:

The amount of rent and the day it is due are both detailed in the lease. Instructions on where and how to pay rent should be made explicit by landlords.

The contract may specify late fees for renters who are late with their rent payments.

Landlords should accept a variety of payment options, including online payments, cheques, and money orders, to make collecting rent easier for tenants.

Eviction Procedures:

Landlords must give renters sufficient written notice before initiating eviction procedures. This notice must detail the grounds for eviction and a fair deadline by which the tenant must comply.

If the tenant still refuses to leave after receiving the eviction notice, the landlord can sue for possession of the property.

Each side makes its argument to the judge in court. The court will issue an eviction order if the landlord wins the case.

Once the court issues an eviction order, the landlord may file for and obtain a writ of possession to reclaim ownership of the property.

Law enforcement may be called in to help the landlord regain ownership of the property and carry out the eviction.

Both landlords and tenants can benefit from a leasing relationship that is legally sound, respectful, and harmonious if they take the time to educate themselves on the rights and responsibilities of each party, the different types of eviction, the essential elements of lease agreements, and the procedures for rent collection and eviction. By following these rules and regulations, landlords and tenants can avoid or resolve any conflicts and have a positive leasing experience.

10.

Property management

Effective property management is essential to the preservation of a property's value, its capacity to fulfill its intended purpose, and its potential to generate a profit in the fast-paced and competitive real estate industry. This chapter digs into the complex realm of property management, illuminating the myriad of complexities and obligations that are linked with the oversight of real estate holdings.

Property management is a broad subject that involves a wide range of tasks, ranging from ensuring the properties are in good physical condition to fostering pleasant relationships between landlords and tenants. The complexities of property management agreements, which are legal documents that establish the connection that exists between property owners and management entities, are investigated in this chapter.

One of the most important aspects of property management is making sure that buildings and grounds are properly maintained and repaired. Property managers not only increase the properties' market worth by preserving the properties' physical integrity, but they also assure the safety of the residents and increase their level of happiness.

The relationship between the landlord and the tenant is one of the most important aspects of property management. This chapter digs into ways for encouraging positive interactions while also handling any conflicts that may develop. As a means to maintain amicable relationships between landlords and tenants, many strategies for improving communication, ensuring tenants comply with lease requirements, and mediating disagreements are being investigated.

The administration of the company's finances is an essential component of property management. This chapter goes deep into the complexities of operating and trust accounts, illuminating how money is managed to meet property bills, maintenance, and other financial components of the business.

Compliance with fair housing rules, which ensure that all individuals have equal access to housing possibilities, is an essential component of property management that should not be overlooked. This chapter offers insights into these regulations and their implications for property managers. It emphasizes how important it is to avoid discrimination and to treat everyone the same.

This chapter, in its essence, offers a complete investigation into property management as an important function within the real estate business. This chapter equips readers with a deep understanding of the complexities and responsibilities associated with effectively managing real estate properties by delving into property management agreements, maintenance and repairs, landlord-tenant relationships, financial management, and fair housing laws. Additionally, the chapter provides readers with an overview of fair housing laws.

Property Management

In the field of real estate, property management is a comprehensive profession that entails supervising and maintaining properties on behalf of property owners. This is done on behalf of the property management company. Property managers play an essential part in maintaining the value of real estate assets while also ensuring that they work properly and generate a profit. Property management encompasses a diverse range of properties, each of which presents its own set of issues and requirements. These can range from residential complexes to commercial structures. To effectively manage property, one needs a combination of organizational abilities, communication skills, financial acumen, and a comprehensive awareness of both the legal and operational sides of property management.

Property managers are responsible for acting as middlemen between property owners and tenants, with the goals of fostering open communication and meeting the requirements of both groups. They are responsible for a variety of tasks, including as tenant screening, lease administration, rent collecting, coordination of maintenance, and resolution of disputes. Property management includes not only the control of the physical property, but also the administration of finances, the compliance with regulations, and the cultivation of positive relationships in order to assure the continued profitability of the properties that are under management over the long term.

Property Management Agreements

Property management agreements are contracts that are legally enforceable and that codify the connection between property owners and property management firms or individual property managers. These agreements can be made between individual property managers and property management businesses. These agreements provide a clear structure for how the property will be administered, including the rights, obligations, and expectations of both parties involved in the transaction. A property management agreement can look very different depending on a number of different aspects, including the type of property being managed, the services that are being provided, and the particular conditions that were negotiated between the owner and the management business.

The scope of services, the management fees, the duration of the agreement, the termination provisions, the duties for maintenance and repairs, the rent collecting procedures, and the financial reporting requirements are key components of property management agreements. The agreement provides as a plan for how the property manager would handle various areas of property management, such as promoting the property, selecting tenants, handling unexpected repairs, and preserving financial records.

Property management agreements offer legal protection to both property owners and property managers. These agreements ensure that expectations are clearly defined and that conflicts may be addressed based on the terms that were previously agreed upon. These agreements encourage transparency, responsibility, and professionalism in the working relationships between property management companies.

Property Maintenance and Repairs

Maintenance and repairs are essential elements of efficient property management because of the direct impact they have on the state of the property, the level of satisfaction experienced by tenants, and the total value of the investment. Property managers are accountable for ensuring that the properties under their care are well-maintained, secure, and in accordance with any applicable legislation. Tenant retention can be improved through regular maintenance and rapid repairs, which also help to reduce the risk of costly problems and uphold the property's reputation.

The term "maintenance" refers to day-to-day responsibilities like mowing the lawn, sweeping the common spaces, and repairing broken or worn down components. Inspections at regular intervals help uncover potential issues before they become more serious. The lifespan of property components can be extended by the implementation of preventative maintenance methods such as servicing of HVAC systems and inspections of roofs, which can also minimize the costs of unforeseen repairs.

On the other side, repairs are used to resolve problems that have suddenly arisen or are the result of tenant neglect. Property managers have a responsibility to respond quickly to requests for repairs and to cooperate with certified contractors to guarantee timely and effective solutions. During the course of the repair process, it is essential to maintain open lines of communication with the renters in order to effectively manage their expectations and avoid disturbances.

For the purpose of catering to a variety of upkeep and repair requirements, property managers should build a trustworthy network of contractors, vendors, and service providers. It is critical for property owners to create a maintenance and repair budget, as this assists them in allocating funds for the continuing care of their properties.

Property managers may improve tenant satisfaction, maintain property value, and contribute to a favorable reputation for both the managed property and the management company as a whole by taking preventative measures to manage maintenance and repairs. Effective maintenance and repair procedures are the cornerstones of successful property management. These procedures ensure that properties continue to be aesthetically pleasing, fulfill their intended purposes, and are in accordance with applicable regulatory standards.

Landlord-Tenant Relationships and Dispute Resolution

Relationships between landlords and tenants are essential to the management of rental properties because they have a significant impact on tenant happiness, property value, and the overall profitability of real estate investments. For the management of these relationships to be successful, there must be open communication, transparency, and a proactive attitude to resolving any potential problems that may crop up.

Communication: Putting in place open channels of communication is of the utmost importance. Tenants who have questions, concerns, or requests for maintenance should be able to communicate with the property manager through a variety of different channels. Timely replies not only indicate a dedication to the happiness of the tenants but also have the potential to stop even relatively minor problems from becoming more serious.

Management of Leases: Property managers are responsible for ensuring that lease agreements are thorough and describe the rights and duties of both parties. Clear rental obligations eliminate the potential for misunderstandings and help set the stage for a cordial working relationship.

The resolution of conflicts is important in landlord-tenant interactions since disagreements are unavoidable. The conflict resolution processes that property managers put in place should be as efficient as possible. Resolving issues in a timely and equitable manner can help preserve the loyalty of tenants and reduce the likelihood of legal confrontations.

Screening Potential Tenants A comprehensive tenant screening process helps reduce the likelihood of having troublesome tenants. Property managers can identify tenants who are more likely to fulfill their duties under a lease by conducting background checks, evaluating credit, and contacting references.

Inspections on a Routine Basis Property managers are able to uncover maintenance issues and handle tenant compliance with lease requirements when they perform inspections on their properties on a regular basis. These inspections have the potential to avert possible conflicts and guarantee that renters are abiding by the regulations governing the property.

Operating and Trust - How to Manage Money

Management of the property's finances is an essential component of property management. Property managers are responsible for a variety of financial transactions, the upkeep of correct records, and the proper administration of the monies in their charge.

Operating and Trust Accounts: In most cases, property managers are responsible for maintaining both operating and trust accounts. The day-to-day costs associated with the property are covered by the operating accounts, while the security deposits and rent that was pre-paid are held in the trust accounts. By keeping these accounts separate from one another, you can ensure that you are in compliance with the legal requirements and prevent the mixing of funds.

Tracking Expenses Property managers are responsible for keeping an accurate record of all income and expenses connected to the property. The ability to provide accurate financial reports and maintain transparency with property owners is made possible by keeping detailed records.

Creating and sticking to a budget is an extremely important part of responsible financial management. Property managers are responsible for forecasting recurring expenditures, setting aside funds for building upkeep and repairs, and budgeting for unforeseen costs.

Rent Collection: Effective rent collection procedures guarantee a consistent flow of income into your business. Property managers have a responsibility to effectively communicate when rent payments are due, offer tenants a variety of payment methods, and take timely action to handle overdue balances.

Reporting Financial Information: In order to keep track of how their properties are performing, property owners rely heavily on reliable financial information. Financial statements should be provided on a regular basis by property managers. These statements should detail income, spending, and any outstanding balances.

Fair Housing Laws

There are rules and regulations in place to avoid discrimination in housing transactions called fair housing laws and regulations. Property managers have a responsibility to comply with these rules in order to guarantee that all individuals have equal access to housing opportunities.

Fair housing rules ban discrimination on the basis of protected characteristics such race, color, religion, sex, national origin, disability, and familial status. Other protected qualities include national origin, disability, and familial status.

Advertising and Tenant Selection: It is imperative that property managers steer clear of any terminology that could be construed as discriminatory when it comes to advertising and tenant selection. The tenant screening criteria should be used in the same manner to each and every applicant.

Rental Property Managers are Required to Provide Reasonable Accommodations Property managers are required to provide reasonable accommodations for disabled tenants. Among these options is the possibility of making alterations to the property in order to improve accessibility.

Training on Fair Housing Property managers and staff members should participate in frequent fair housing training in order to remain up to date on the most recent rules and the best methods for complying with them.

Regarding the reporting: It is critical to comply with fair housing regulations. In order to establish compliance with fair housing standards, property managers are required to keep documents relating to tenant applications, decisions regarding leasing, and communication.

11.

Transfer of title

• ———————————— •

The transfer of title is a critical junction in the complex web of real estate deals. Fundamental to all real estate deals is the transfer of legal title from one buyer to another through this procedure. This chapter sets off on an in-depth investigation of the various facets of the transfer of title, illuminating the complex legal systems, safeguards, and nuanced considerations that create this vital aspect of the real estate market.

The first step in exploring this vast area is reading some deeds and learning about the role they play in transferring ownership. Each sort of deed, from the broad protection afforded by general warranty deeds to the narrow transfers effected by quitclaim deeds, serves as tangible documentation of the transfer of ownership.

After an introduction, the chapter digs into the minute details of a title search and a title insurance policy. A property's history can be clouded by claims, liens, or encumbrances that are revealed by a title search. Title insurance protects against unforeseen claims, easing the transfer process and lowering the stakes.

However, there are obstacles in the way of property transfers. Disputes over ownership can arise if there are "clouds on title," or ambiguities or encumbrances. Methods for settling such disagreements and clearing up any ambiguities about ownership are discussed in this chapter.

More research elucidates the variation between marketable and insurable titles, highlighting the significance of both in a transfer. Having an unclouded title is essential when selling a home, and title insurance provides an extra degree of security.

This chapter examines what makes a dee, the central document in the transfer procedure, a valid one. To make sure the transfer is legal and enforceable, you need to be aware of these factors.

In-depth analysis of the most common kinds of deeds reveals their variety and specificity. This analysis helps readers better grasp the differences between general warranty deeds and more specific quitclaim deeds.

This chapter recognizes the specific dynamics at play in the arena of distressed properties such as short sales, foreclosures, and real estate owned (REO) properties, and it reveals the complications of transfer within these contexts.

Home warranties provide peace of mind for buyers by covering the cost of maintenance and replacements for systems and appliances that may break down during the sale of a home.

This chapter guides you through the landmines of escrow and closing procedures, clearing the air as you near the end of your property's ownership transfer. There is also a focus on the money side of things, with advice on how to figure out your closing costs and how to prorate them fairly.

The chapter concludes with an examination of the tax consequences inherent in the sale or purchase of real estate, placing special emphasis on the larger financial landscape and factors to be considered by both buyers and sellers.

This chapter explores the complex world of property title transfers and provides readers with a thorough familiarity with the laws, safeguards, and nuanced considerations that govern such transactions. This investigation equips stakeholders with clarity, foresight, and confidence to negotiate the complex arena of real estate by traversing title conveyance, deeds, title searches, insurance, disputes, and the various elements of property transfer.

Title Conveyance and Deeds

Conveyance of title is the most important step in the process of transferring property ownership. The "deed" is the key legal document in this transaction. Deeds are physical evidence of the transfer of ownership, cementing the legal agreement between the grantor (seller) and the grantee (buyer). The importance of this action in transferring legal ownership of the property to the buyer cannot be emphasized.

There are several varieties of deeds, each one designed to address a particular situation and providing varying degrees of security and guarantees. One of the most thorough is the "general warranty deed," which affords the grantee the greatest possible protection. This deed protects the grantor against any claims made by prior owners and ensures that the grantor has good title. On the other hand, a "quitclaim deed" conveys the grantor's interest in the property in its current form, without any representations or guarantees. Common examples are divorce settlements and the transfer of property between relatives.

It takes particular components for a deed to be recognized by the law. For example:

The individual transferring the property must have the mental and legal capacity to make the transfer.

A precise and exhaustive description of the property should be included in the deed.

The grantor's aim to convey property must be made crystal apparent in the deed's language.

The grantee must be named in the deed as the person or entity receiving the property.

Signing by the Grantor: The grantor's signature is required on the deed.

In real estate transactions, the choice of deed type is crucial since it establishes the scope of the grantee's protections and guarantees. To ensure a safe and efficient transfer of ownership, it is crucial for all parties to fully grasp the consequences of each deed type.

Title Search and Title Insurance

A thorough title search is performed before a property's ownership may be transferred in order to learn about the property's previous owners and uncover any problems that can arise with the title. The smooth transfer of ownership depends on this procedure being completed to provide a "clean title," one that is free from encumbrances, liens, or claims. In order to trace the history of ownership, a title search examines documents including deeds, mortgages, and court filings.

Buyers' interests are further protected by title insurance. This safeguards the buyer after the title search has been completed and any claims have been investigated. Owner's title insurance and lender's title insurance are the two most common kinds of title protection. Lender's title insurance safeguards the mortgage lender's interest in the property, whereas owner's title insurance protects the buyer's financial investment in the property.

Clouds on Title and Ownership Disputes

It is possible for "clouds on title" to arise even after a comprehensive title search and the issuing of title insurance, which could lead to a dispute over the property's ownership. Any claim, lien, or encumbrance that causes a cloud on title must be resolved before the property can be owned free and clear. Unresolved liens, border disputes, and forged documents are just a few examples of the many potential causes of this type of problem.

When more than one person claims ownership of an item, or when there is any doubt as to who the true owner is, a dispute over ownership is possible. Such disagreements can cause the transfer of ownership to be severely delayed or disrupted, leading to legal fights and financial losses for both parties.

For clouded titles and ownership conflicts, the courts will often resort to "quiet title actions," which aim to clear the title by removing any and all claims to the land in question. Disputes can be resolved and a smooth transfer of ownership can be accomplished through settlement negotiations between the parties.

Title Requirements - Marketable vs Insurable

The ideas of marketable and insurable title are of utmost importance in the complicated world of property ownership. Each of these phrases has specific ramifications for the safety and ease with which property ownership can be transferred.

The title to your property must be free and clear of any liens, encumbrances, or other legal issues that could prevent you from selling it. A marketable title indicates that all questions regarding the property's ownership have been resolved and that the property is free and clear to be sold. Titles that are free and clear of any liens or other legal encumbrances make a piece of real estate more appealing to potential buyers.

However, a title is considered "insurable" if and only if it satisfies the requirements of a title insurance provider. A title that is insurable means that the title insurance company is willing to give protection against claims or flaws, but this does not ensure a defect-free title. Title insurance provides a safety net in the event of title problems, protecting both purchasers and lenders.

The difference between titles that can be sold and those that can be insured is nuanced but crucial. The absence of any flaws in the title is the most important factor in making it saleable. An insurable title considers whether or not a title insurance company is ready to take on the risks of any title problems. Although having a marketable title is essential for a claim-free transfer of ownership, having an insurable title provides an additional degree of security.

The Essential Elements of a Valid Deed

The transfer of property ownership from one party to another is facilitated by a lawful deed, which is a fundamental legal instrument. To make sure the transfer is lawful and enforceable, it's important to know what constitutes a valid deed.

The individual executing the deed must be both legally able to transfer the property and of sound mind.

Intent of Grantor: The deed must make it crystal obvious that the grantor intends to transfer ownership.

Accurate and complete information about the property being transferred must be included in the deed. This guarantees that there is no confusion over which asset is being referred to.

The deed's language should make it clear that the grantor is transferring ownership of the property to the grantee.

The grantee must be named in the deed so that it is clear who is taking title to the property.

The term "consideration" is used to describe the value that was given or received in the transfer. Although money is the most common kind of exchange, other forms of value or promises may also be involved.

The grantor's signature and date on the deed are required for execution and delivery. For a deed to be legally binding, it may be necessary to have witnesses or a notary sign it.

Each of these components is essential to the validity of the deed and, by extension, the ownership transfer. Any deed missing one of these components may be challenged as invalid, which could lead to legal trouble.

Transfer of Ownership - The Main Types of Deeds

Deeds are legal documents used to formally transfer ownership of real property. Deeds can provide various levels of protection and warranties to the grantee. Buyers and sellers need to be familiar with the most common deed kinds to ensure that the transfer procedure meets their needs and expectations.

The grantee is afforded the most security under a general warranty deed. The grantor unconditionally guarantees and warrants the property against all claims from prior owners. This deed guarantees that the property being conveyed to the grantee is free and clear of any liens or claims.

While similar to a general warranty deed, a special warranty deed provides protection only from claims that become effective during the grantor's possession. Claims made before the grantor acquired the property are not covered.

The assurances and guarantees provided by the previous two deeds are not present in a quitclaim deed. It conveys to the grantee the grantor's entire interest in the property. Non-sale transactions, such as those involving family members or in the context of divorce, may include the use of a quitclaim deed.

Trade and Bargaining This deed delivers property to the grantee without any guarantees, although it does imply that the grantor is legally able to do so. This does not provide assurance that the property is claim-free.

There are several kinds of deeds for different situations, such as a gift deed for the purpose of making a gift of property, a sheriff's deed after a foreclosure auction, and a trustee's deed for the purpose of holding property in trust.

Different deeds provide differing degrees of security to the grantee and are used for various purposes. The transfer of ownership should be in accordance with the intents and expectations of the parties, therefore selecting the proper type of deed is crucial.

Transferring Distressed Properties - Short Sales, Foreclosures, & REO

Short sales, foreclosures, and real estate owned (REO) transactions are all types of distressed properties that provide distinct issues and obstacles when transferring ownership.

To put it simply, a short sale is when a homeowner sells their home for less than what is still owed on the mortgage. Lender consent to sale is required, and debt is often settled through discussions. Negotiations with the seller and the lender can get complicated during a short sale's transfer of ownership.

When a borrower stops making their mortgage payments, the lender can legally reclaim the property through a process known as foreclosure. In order to recoup the loan, the lender will often auction off the property. In a foreclosure, ownership is transferred to whoever pays the most money at auction; if no one does, the lender takes possession.

If a foreclosure auction doesn't bring a buyer, the lender may take possession of the property and list it as real estate owned (REO). The lender takes title to the property and tries to sell it the old fashioned way. An REO sale's transfer of ownership functions similarly to any other transaction, with the exception that the seller in this case is the lender.

Legal constraints, negotiations, and the involvement of lenders all add complication to the transfer of foreclosed homes. Prospective purchasers of foreclosed homes need to understand these nuances to complete a smooth purchase of a property in trouble.

Home Warranties

Repair costs for your house's major systems and appliances are covered by a home warranty, a service contract. A house warranty is similar to but separate from homeowner's insurance in that it primarily addresses the property's mechanical systems and appliances rather than its structural components. Both homebuyers and sellers may rest easy knowing that their investment is protected against the high expense of unforeseen repairs thanks to a home warranty.

Important features of house warranties are:

Warranties for homes often include protection for heating, ventilation, air conditioning, plumbing, electrical, and appliance systems including dishwashers, microwaves, and clothes washers and dryers. It's possible that covering for such things is an available add-on.

Home warranties typically last for one year, but can be renewed for another. Once the property's transfer of ownership is finalized, the coverage term will begin.

of the event of a breakdown of a covered system or appliance, the homeowner notifies the warranty company, who then dispatches a service personnel to the home.

Costs: Home warranties need an up-front payment from the buyer, seller, or both. In addition, every time a technician is sent out, there may be a service call cost incurred.

Coverage limitations, exclusions, and maximum repair or replacement costs are common in home warranty contracts. Read the fine print to find out what is and isn't covered.

Home warranties are an attractive selling advantage because they can be transferred to the new owner in the case of a property sale.

Buyers can receive peace of mind during the first few years of ownership with financial protection from costly repairs that might arise without a home warranty. Home warranties are a great way for sellers to reassure buyers and increase interest in their listing

Escrow and Closing Procedures- Completing the Transfer of Ownership

Closing and Escrow Procedures: Completing the Ownership Transfer

When purchasing real estate, it is common practice to have a third party act as an escrow agent to hold payments and paperwork until certain terms are fulfilled. The final phase of a property sale or purchase is the closing, often called the settlement. Closing and escrow procedures guarantee that all responsibilities are met, money is dispersed accurately, and contracts are signed.

Escrow and closing processes consist primarily of the following:

A title search is performed prior to closing to guarantee a free and clear title, and title insurance is purchased if necessary. The purpose of title insurance is to safeguard the lender and the buyer from any unanticipated claims.

If the buyer needs a loan to pay for the acquisition, that loan must be approved before the closing can take place.

Usually, the buyer will do one last walk-through of the property before closing to make sure everything is in order and according to the contract.

The Closing Disclosure is a document that specifies the loan's final terms and any associated fees. At least three working days before to the closing, it must be delivered to the buyer.

The closing meeting is where the deed, mortgage, and other legal agreements are signed by the buyer and seller.

Distribution of Funds: The Escrow Holder releases Funds Per Agreement Terms. Everything must be paid, from the seller's commission to the real estate brokers' fees and more.

The final step in transferring ownership is recording the deed with the relevant government agency when all the necessary paperwork has been signed and the money has been dispersed.

The purpose of the escrow and closing processes is to facilitate a smooth and lawful transfer of ownership. The closing is the last step in the process of buying a home or other property and the beginning of a new chapter in the lives of both the buyer and the seller.

Calculating Closing Costs

Generally speaking, the buyer is responsible for closing fees, however, the seller may be required to contribute to the total amount. These expenses extend beyond the initial price tag to include a variety of add-ons and administration charges.

The following are typical parts of the closing costs:

The costs associated with a loan include things like the cost of getting a credit report, an assessment, and the interest rate.

Included in these costs are those necessary to guarantee a clean title, such as title insurance, title search fees, and title settlement costs.

Fees charged by an escrow business typically include the cost of keeping funds and managing the closure.

Fees charged by the government, such as recording costs, transfer taxes, and property tax assessments that have already been paid.

Escrow accounts for property taxes, homeowners insurance, and mortgage insurance are examples of prepaid items.

Fees for house inspections include the price of any necessary pest inspections.

Lawyer Costs: Money paid to a lawyer to have them look over contracts and provide you advice.

Surveys, HOA dues, and other miscellaneous costs may be added to a transaction's total price tag, depending on the property's location and the terms of the sale.

Both buyers and sellers need to know how much money will be changing hands, so it's important to figure out closing fees. A Loan Estimate (LE) and a Closing Disclosure (CD) are two documents commonly used to offer estimates of closing costs to all parties involved.

Proration: Allocating Expenses

Proration is a method for equitably dividing up costs between a buyer and a seller based on the respective lengths of their periods of ownership during a given time frame. Sharing the burden of maintaining the property is kept equitable through the use of prorations.

Proration is typically applied to recurring costs like property taxes, HOA dues, and utility bills. This is how proration is calculated:

Taxes on real estate are often split proportionally between the buyer and seller based on when the transaction occurs in the fiscal year. The party that owns the property on the tax assessment date must pay all taxes for that year, and the other party must reimburse the first party for the time they actually had possession of the property.

Similar to property taxes, HOA dues are calculated on a prorated basis based on the date of ownership. The buyer assumes responsibility for the remaining months, while the seller is responsible for the months they actually lived in the home.

Water and electric bills are prorated so that both parties pay their fair share depending on their respective periods of ownership.

With proration in place, the onus of paying recurring costs is fairly distributed between the buyer and the supplier. This avoids situations in which one party is responsible for costs incurred before or after their period of ownership.

Tax Implications of Property Transfer

There are often major tax consequences for both parties involved in a property transfer. If you want to make smart financial decisions and steer clear of any unpleasant tax surprises, you need to be aware of these ramifications.

Among the most important tax factors are:

Transfer taxes are levied on the sale or transfer of property and are imposed by some states and municipal governments. Both the buyer and the seller may be responsible for these taxes depending on local regulations.

Any profit made by a seller on the sale of property may be liable to capital gains tax. If certain conditions are met, including those related to ownership and use, then primary residences may be exempt.

By investing the profits of a sale into another property of the same sort, a seller can avoid paying capital gains tax under Section 1031 of the Internal Revenue Code. This type of transaction is known as a 1031 exchange and is governed by strict regulations and time limits.

Taxes on real estate may be lowered or raised depending on the property's assessed value and the applicable tax rate. These modifications may affect the seller's prorated duties at closing as well as the buyer's ongoing tax liabilities.

Mortgage interest and property tax payments made by the buyer and seller may be deducted by the Internal Revenue Service.

Transferring property involves tax ramifications that should be carefully considered, usually with the assistance of tax professionals or financial consultants. If buyers and sellers are aware of these tax implications, they will be better able to make decisions that are in line with their long-term financial objectives.

12.

Practice For Real Estate

———•———•———

Responsibility, ethics, communication, and competence weave the real estate sector. This chapter explores the complex real estate industry. Each course covers a crucial part of real estate agents' jobs, from creating relationships through efficient communication to handling technology, laws, and ethics.

Real estate deals depend on good communication. Engaging, understanding, and communicating is an art. Communicators build trust, allay fears, and educate clients and customers throughout the real estate process. Active listening, adjusting communication styles, and clear, empathetic communication are stressed in this chapter.

Real estate professionals' fiduciary duty is highlighted via trust and escrow accounts. These accounts require precise management, transparency, and legal compliance to protect client finances. This chapter discusses trust and escrow account responsibilities, stressing financial stewardship and client fund accountability.

Real estate is based on fairness and equality, and it has made progress against discrimination. Blockbusting, steering, and redlining perpetuate bias and discrimination and are illegal. This chapter emphasizes the need for a non-discriminatory real estate environment. Professionals help ensure fair housing for all by following fair housing rules, which prohibit discrimination based on race, religion, handicap, and more.

Real estate requires knowledge of both forbidden and authorized behaviors and exclusions under fair housing regulations. Ethical and legal practice requires balancing compliance and justified exclusions. This chapter emphasizes legal compliance and educated decision-making.

Technology has expanded marketing and advertising in the digital age. Digital tools have transformed property marketing, transactions, and client engagement. This chapter discusses how professionals use technology and digital marketing ethics.

Real estate negotiation requires diplomacy, strategy, and empathy. This chapter explains how experts can negotiate agreements that benefit all parties. Real estate professionals achieve successful and fair negotiations by collaborating and maintaining relationships.

Technology has revolutionized the real estate industry. Virtual property tours and digital contracts have improved client experiences and streamlined operations. This chapter examines the digital tools and resources that enable professionals to adapt, connect, and succeed in a fast changing market.

Real estate ethics go beyond legality. Every choice is based on ethics, transparency, and client interests. This chapter discusses the ethics of the profession and the importance of credibility and trust in all interactions.

Real estate professionals have many employment models, each with its own salary, responsibilities, and obligations. This chapter explains how professionals can participate in the industry, helping them choose a career.

Due diligence is essential for agents navigating real estate deals. Agents educate clients about property history and zoning laws. This chapter emphasizes professional due diligence.

Client needs and transaction dynamics determine real estate agents' varied duties. Each role—buyer's agent, seller's agent, transaction coordinator, etc.—requires a customized approach.

Finally, antitrust rules emphasize the need for a fair and competitive real estate market. These regulations ensure fair competition and prevent anti-competitive practices in the industry.

Effective Communication with Clients and Customers

When it comes to real estate, effective communication goes beyond just talking; it also involves listening, comprehending on an emotional level, and adjusting to different communication styles. Professionals can make better decisions on behalf of their clients if they practice active listening and pay close attention to their feedback. For difficult ideas to be understood by all parties involved, clear expression is crucial. By connecting with the customer on an emotional level, you can gain their trust and get their business. Effective involvement is guaranteed by accommodating many modes of communication. Video conversations and other forms of digital communication are improving the quality of virtual interactions and lending a more human dimension to online business. In conclusion, experts in the field can better serve their clients by mastering the art of clear and compassionate communication.

Trust / Escrow Accounts - Agent Responsibilities

Escrow and trust accounts, which contain fiduciary duties towards customers, play a crucial role in the real estate industry. The monies in these accounts are managed in a transparent and responsible manner by real estate experts, who make timely deposits and keep correct records. Accountability and trust are fostered when clients can see how their money is being spent. Escrow services are third-party intermediaries that help keep business dealings honest and secure. Clients' financial interests are protected when advisors follow the rules and steer clear of conflicts of interest. Agents who are associated with brokerages should study their processes to make sure they are following the law and acting ethically. Professionals' dedication to their clients' financial well-being is reflected in their ethical behavior, legal compliance, and stewardship of trust and escrow accounts.

Blockbusting, Steering, and Redlining - Prohibited Conduct

Reprehensible discriminatory methods such as blockbusting, steering, and redlining are prohibited. For financial gain, the blockbusting industry plays on people's fears by proposing racial changes in residential areas. Clients are steered depending on their demographics, thus cementing their isolation. Redlining is the practice of rejecting loans to people based on the appearance of their area. These policies go against the spirit of inclusion and fair housing. To ensure that everyone has access to affordable housing, it is essential to recognize and avoid these practices.

Fair Housing Laws - Protected Classes

The Fair Housing Act and other similar fair housing regulations are essential to achieving this goal. Discrimination on the basis of race, color, religion, national origin, sexual orientation, disability, or familial status is prohibited. All customers must be treated the same, regardless of any legally protected traits, in order to comply with these regulations. The commitment to equality in the real estate sector goes well beyond what is required by law; it requires self-awareness and education to reduce bias and foster an inclusive housing market.

Acts and Exemptions

Knowing what kinds of conduct are illegal and what kinds of situations are protected from these rules is crucial for anyone dealing with fair housing issues. Refusal to rent or sell, setting differing terms or conditions, or providing false information about availability all fall under the category of prohibited discriminatory activities. However, exemptions recognize cases where certain requirements are met and permit limited exclusions. Some senior citizen residences, for instance, may have restrictions based on family composition. The difficulty lies in negotiating these nuances without compromising the principles underlying fair housing legislation. In order to perform ethically and legally, professionals must be aware of what is forbidden and when exceptions apply.

Marketing and Advertising Strategies

The real estate industry's use of marketing and advertising methods has been revolutionized by the digital age. The audience for real estate commercials has grown thanks to the proliferation of online portals, social media, virtual tours, and customized marketing. Marketing isn't only about showing products; it's also about conveying a story, appealing to customers' emotions, and forging meaningful relationships. The effectiveness of messages can be increased by learning about the intended receivers and adapting them accordingly. When it comes to ethics, nothing is more important than being honest and forthright while also being accurate in your portrayal of people and situations. Finding that sweet spot between originality and genuineness in your marketing can give your efforts the credibility and integrity they deserve.

Negotiation Techniques and Strategies

The art of negotiation is akin to a dance requiring dexterity, comprehension, and strategic planning. Finding common ground and understanding each party's motivations are crucial to a successful negotiation. Professionals should be able to effectively represent their clients' best interests while working together with them. When experts have empathy and listen attentively, they are able to get to the heart of their clients' problems and come up with original answers. Using win-win scenarios, having well-defined goals, and maintaining composure and patience are all essential components of successful bargaining. Communication that is open and honest fosters trust and establishes credibility. Mastery of negotiation as an art form and a skill sets the stage for agreements that benefit all parties involved.

Real Estate Technology and Digital Tools

Real estate deals have been transformed by technological advancements. Potential purchasers can take a virtual tour of a property without physically visiting it, and digital contracts reduce administrative hassles. Market and consumer preferences can be better understood with the help of data analytics. Mobile apps allow for instantaneous interaction and teamwork. Acceptance of technology, however, necessitates striking a harmony between effectiveness and warmth. While digital tools improve reach and convenience, they shouldn't replace experts' one-on-one counsel. Technology-savvy professionals improve interactions with customers and thrive in a dynamic business environment.

Ethical Considerations in Real Estate Practice

Integrity is the bedrock of any successful real estate career. Maintaining honesty, openness, and responsibility as benchmarks is crucial. When serving a customer, professionals must put their client's needs first, even if those needs are at odds with their own. Ethical responsibilities include truthfulness in reporting, impartiality in making decisions, and secrecy in dealing with sensitive material. Professionals are expected to deal with ethical quandaries in an open and forthright manner. Dealing with customers, coworkers, and the general public all require a high level of ethical discernment. Following moral guidelines helps build credibility, strengthens connections, and boosts standing in the marketplace.

Real Estate Agent Employment

Different forms of employment for real estate agents have different ramifications for how they do their jobs. Freelancers determine their own work hours and how they run their businesses. They must pay their own way, though, including all applicable taxes. However, agents who work for brokerages often receive additional benefits, including as education, administrative help, and tools. Agents can better align their career goals and work preferences by learning about the benefits and drawbacks of various employment arrangements.

Due Diligence - Real Estate Agent Scope of Practice

Agents in the real estate industry play a crucial role in assisting customers through the due diligence process so that they may make educated judgments. This include investigating the property's past, as well as zoning laws and other problems. While agents can be a wealth of information, they do have limitations. Working together with professionals like inspectors, appraisers, and lawyers improves due diligence. Agents' responsibilities often include helping customers with research, arranging for inspections, and providing risk assessment advice. Professionalism and thoroughness are bolstered by practitioners who are aware of their own limitations and who seek out the help of specialists when necessary.

General Real Estate Agent Job Duties

As mediators between buyers and sellers, real estate brokers have many responsibilities. Real estate pricing relies heavily on market research. Market and property characteristics need to be considered when assigning a value to a property. During listing presentations, prospective buyers are shown around the houses for sale. Clients rely on agents to help them negotiate contracts, handle unforeseen events, and coordinate business deals. Agents must maintain open lines of communication with their customers by responding to their inquiries and concerns. It is crucial to keep abreast of the latest market tendencies, legal mandates, and industry advancements. Agents' work helps transactions go smoothly, keeps clients' interests safe, and builds confidence.

Different Roles of a Real Estate Agent

To best serve their clients, real estate brokers often wear many hats. A buyer's agent acts as an advocate for the buyer, helping them find the right property and securing the best possible terms. A seller's agent is a real estate professional whose duties include advertising, showing, and negotiating the sale of a property. When it comes to paperwork and timelines, transaction coordinators are the ones in charge. When an agent represents two sides of a transaction, full disclosure and compliance with the law are essential. Real estate brokers sometimes specialize in one area, such as high-end homes, commercial properties, or property management. Agents who are aware of their respective functions are better able to meet their customers' needs.

Antitrust Laws

Competition is encouraged and anti-competitive activities that hurt customers are prohibited under antitrust laws. Agents in the real estate industry should never work together with their rivals to manipulate pricing or divide up markets. Price fixing, bid rigging, and coordinated consumer boycotts are all illegal. It is in the best interest of both customers and the market for agents to compete on a level playing field. Knowledge of antitrust laws is essential for maintaining ethical and lawful company activities. Compliance with these regulations is essential to maintaining the real estate industry's commitment to honesty, openness, and trustworthiness.

13.

Real state Calculations

Numbers are crucial in the complicated real estate industry, where they are used in everything from decisions to transactions to valuations. Real estate calculations constitute the backbone of well-informed decisions, from estimating property prices to examining investments. This section digs into the world of real estate mathematics, preparing readers to handle the wide variety of computations that are commonplace in the field. Accurate and insightful real estate calculations require practitioners to have a firm grasp of fundamental mathematical principles, techniques of calculation, and standard instruments. Professionals' ability to succeed in the ever-changing real estate market is bolstered by their facility with statistics, which is essential for a wide range of tasks, including valuing properties, analyzing investments, and overseeing closing expenses.

The T-Bar Method is discussed in these pages, and is shown to be a useful technique for quickly and easily solving difficult mathematical problems. The complexities of converting between percents, decimals, and fractions are removed, allowing for more fluid work with numbers. By delving into the specifics of mortgage payment calculations, we remove the mystery from what is a crucial factor for both buyers and sellers. The techniques used to determine a property's worth are revealed, providing new insight into the foundations of professionally conducted appraisals. We untangle the complex web of tax-related mathematics, including property, transfer, and recording taxes.

Focusing on the examination of investments, we examine methods of calculating returns in order to provide guidance for assessing possible real estate investments. The complexity of proration and closing fees is removed, allowing experts to tackle these challenges with greater ease. An investor's ability to calculate a capitalization rate and a gross rent multiplier is becoming increasingly important for evaluating the prospective profitability of real estate ventures.

The financial sides of real estate transactions, including buyer funds, seller proceeds, and equity calculations, are brought to the foreground. Calculating rental property depreciation also sheds light on the nuances of managing rental properties as a source of income.

We delve into land measuring with an eye on accuracy, providing experts with the tools they need to make reliable measurements of property. The techniques used to measure houses and buildings can shed light on the fundamental feature of property value known as the quantification of structures. The final section of the chapter provides a summary of the most useful online resources for real estate math, allowing professionals to take advantage of modern technologies to streamline and improve their numerical skills.

This chapter sets off on an exploration of real estate calculations, providing readers with the tools they need to effectively use numbers in their fields. Real estate professionals may improve their decision-making, advise their clients more effectively, and successfully traverse the industry's complicated landscape if they have a firm grasp of the requisite mathematical concepts.

Basic Math Concepts

Anyone who works in the real estate industry absolutely has to have a firm grasp of the fundamental mathematical ideas involved. These fundamental concepts serve as the basis for more intricate mathematical computations and analytic procedures. The fundamental concepts underlying real estate mathematics are derived from arithmetic operations such as addition, subtraction, multiplication, and division. Quantifying values, determining proportions, and tracking changes over time can all be accomplished with the help of fundamental numerical representations such as fractions, decimals, and percentages. Calculations are more likely to be accurate when the order of operations is understood.

The T-Bar Method

Calculations that involve a number of different variables can be made much easier by using a sophisticated tool called the T-Bar Method. Practitioners are able to methodically organize and modify information to arrive at correct results if the data is first tabulated and then organized within the table. This method is very helpful for calculating mortgage amortization, analyzing investment performance, and contrasting various potential outcomes. The T-Bar Method helps practitioners to break down complex calculations into manageable parts, so lowering the likelihood of making errors and improving their ability to perform numerical tasks.

Conversions - Percentages, Decimals, and Fractions

Calculations involving real estate always require an understanding of how to convert between percentages, decimals, and fractions. A expert who has mastered these conversions will be able to move fluidly between the various graphical and numerical representations of numerical data. Accurate property value evaluations are made easier, for instance, when one understands that a 25% appreciation is equivalent to a decimal multiplier of 1.25. The process of calculating interest rates, loan periods, and property valuation adjustments all benefits from converting fractions to decimals and percentages. A competent understanding of conversions is necessary for accurate interpretations and computations.

Mortgage Payment Calculations

Calculating monthly mortgage payments is a vital step in the home-buying process for both buyers and sellers. Buyers have the capacity to determine whether or not a mortgage is within their financial means, and sellers gain the ability to gauge the amount of money that could be made. These calculations include the PITI formula, which stands for principle, interest, taxes, and insurance. The amount of the loan, the interest rate, the length of the loan term, and the type of loan all have an impact on the monthly payment. Practitioners who are skilled in the mathematics involved in mortgage payments are able to provide customers with reliable estimates and advise them through decisions that pertain to mortgages.

Property Value Assessment Methods

The importance of making a precise valuation of a property cannot be overstated in the context of real estate transactions. When determining the value of a piece of property, various approaches are taken. The approach known as Comparative Market Analysis (CMA) entails analyzing previous sales of properties that are comparable to the one being considered. The revenue Approach determines the value of a property based on the amount of revenue it is likely to generate in the future. The Cost Approach determines an asset's worth by determining its "replacement cost" and then taking into account its "depreciation" over time.

A practitioner who is proficient in these methodologies is in a position to provide customers with property valuations that are well-informed, which assists buyers and sellers in making decisions that are informed.

Property, Transfer, and Recording Tax Calculations

The property taxes, transfer taxes, and recording taxes that are a part of real estate transactions all have an impact on the parties involved, whether they are purchasers or sellers. Taxes on real estate are recurrent payments made by property owners to the governments of their respective communities in order to finance public services. Transfer taxes are collected whenever ownership of a piece of real estate is transferred to a new individual, whereas recording taxes are levied whenever papers are entered into the public record system. For the purpose of calculating these taxes, a knowledge of the applicable local regulations, assessment values, and tax rates is required. When estimating their clients' tax obligations, professionals are obligated to take into account prorations, exemptions, and deductions. Since accurate tax calculations are vital for both the process of financial planning and the maintenance of compliance with the requirements of the law, they constitute an essential component of the toolkit utilized by real estate professionals.

Investment Analysis and Return Calculations

The possibility of financial gain is the primary motivation behind real estate investments. The process of analyzing an investment is determining whether or not a certain property is economically viable by considering a number of aspects, including its rental revenue, expenses, potential for appreciation, and any tax implications. Calculations of return take into account a variety of indicators, such as the cash-on-cash return, the capitalization rate (cap rate), and the internal rate of return (IRR). The cash-on-cash return is a measure of the initial return on investment, the capitalization rate is an evaluation of the property's revenue in relation to its value, and the internal rate of return is an evaluation of the property's total profitability. These calculations enhance investors' strategic planning for the purpose of maximizing returns and guide investors as they make informed judgments about property acquisitions.

Closing Costs and Proration Calculations

The expenses that are incurred during the final phases of a real estate transaction are referred to as closing costs. The fees associated with title insurance, appraisals, legal services, and other professional services are included in these expenditures. Calculating proration entails dividing monthly costs between the buyer and the seller in proportion to the amount of time each party owned the property during the given month. Common items that are subject to proration include insurance premiums, property taxes, and energy bills. In order to do correct estimates, it is vital to have a solid understanding of the local customs, contract conditions, and methods of proration. It is the responsibility of professionals to give customers with accurate estimates of closing expenses and prorations to ease the process of making informed decisions and to prevent unpleasant financial surprises.

Capitalization Rate and Gross Rent Multiplier Calculation

Both the capitalization rate (cap rate) and the gross rent multiplier (GRM) are important indicators to consider when doing an analysis of real estate investments. The capitalization rate (cap rate) is a measurement of the relationship between the net operating income (NOI) of a property and its market value. When compared to the overall worth of the property, a return that is possibly higher is indicated by a cap rate that is higher. The GRM analyzes the connection between the purchase price of the property and its annual gross rental income. Values of the GRM that are lower are indicative of more earning potential. These calculations provide guidance to investors regarding investment choices and strategies by assisting them in determining the profitability of income-generating properties.

Buyer Funds

It is essential for real estate agents as well as their clients to have a solid understanding of the buyer's financial situation. The term "buyer funds" refers to the financial resources that are necessary to successfully close a real estate deal. This includes the initial deposit, the earnest money deposit, the closing charges, and any possible escrow funds. When calculating buyer funds, it is important to take into consideration the purchase price, the financing conditions, the needs of the lender, and the terms of the contract. The professionals have a responsibility to communicate openly with the customers in order to ensure that the customers are fully informed of their monetary commitments. Clients are able to more effectively manage their budgets, steer clear of unpleasant surprises, and ensure a smoother transaction process when accurate assessments of buyer money are used

Seller Proceeds

It is crucial for sellers as well as real estate professionals to have a solid understanding of seller proceeds. The amount of money left over for the seller after subtracting all of the costs associated with the selling of a property is known as the seller proceeds. These charges include any outstanding mortgage balances or liens, commissions owed to real estate agents, closing costs, and any other real estate-related fees. To accurately calculate seller proceeds, a full understanding of the property's worth, the seller's current commitments, and the expenditures associated with the transaction is required. Real estate specialists play an essential part in ensuring that sellers have a comprehensive comprehension of their financial results, supplying sellers with realistic estimates, and leading them through the process of selling their properties. Real estate professionals contribute to the smooth and profitable completion of deals by precisely determining the proceeds retained by the seller.

Calculating Equity

In the real estate industry, one of the most important ideas is known as equity. Equity is defined as the difference between the current market value of a property and any outstanding mortgage balances. Homeowners who want to understand their current financial position and potential options, such as selling their property or refinancing their mortgage, absolutely need to calculate their equity. To determine the amount of equity in a property, take its current market value and deduct the amount still owed on any outstanding mortgages. A homeowner's ability to make educated financial decisions and utilize the value of their property for a variety of reasons is greatly enhanced by an awareness of equity. Clients might benefit from the assistance of real estate specialists in gaining a grasp of equity and exploring solutions to make the most of their financial situations.

Rental Property Calculations

Calculations pertaining to rental properties are an essential part of examining properties that generate income. Investors can use these calculations to determine whether or not a rental property has the potential to be profitable. Cash flow, gross rental income, and net operating income (NOI) are some of the most important measures. The total money generated by the property before deducting any expenses is known as the property's gross rental income. By deducting operational expenses from gross income, net operating income (NOI) provides a more accurate depiction of the financial performance of the property. Cash flow is the amount of surplus revenue that is still available after all expenditures, such as mortgage payments, have been subtracted from total income. Gaining expertise in the mathematics related to rental properties equips investors with the ability to assess opportunities, determine rent pricing, and make decisions based on data.

Determining Rental Property Depreciation

A tax benefit known as depreciation enables owners of rental properties to reduce their taxable income by an amount equal to a fraction of the property's value over the course of time. Determining the amount of depreciation that should be applied to a rental property requires knowledge of the property's basis (its purchase price), the value of the land, and the applicable depreciation procedures. The Modified Accelerated Cost Recovery System (MACRS) is the form of real estate depreciation that is used the most frequently for residential properties. Using this approach, the cost of the property is spread out over 27.5 years. The decrease in taxable revenue that results from depreciation also results in an increase in cash flow for property owners. Real estate specialists should have a working grasp of depreciation standards in order to assist investors in developing tax strategies that are most advantageous to them.

Land Measurement

Accurate land measurement is essential for both the purchasing and selling of real estate as well as the valuation of properties. The process of quantifying the dimensions of a property's land area is referred to as land measurement. This information is essential for determining property values, evaluating the possibility for development, and adhering to the restrictions that govern zoning. Legal descriptions, surveys, and public records are all types of methods that can be used to measure land. Professionals in the real estate industry need to be familiar with these methodologies and have the ability to assess land measuring data. Accurate land measurement ensures that property values are assessed accurately and that land usage corresponds to local legislation. Accurate land measurement can also help prevent environmental damage.

Homes and Buildings: Measuring Structures

Accurate home and building measurements are essential in real estate deals, property appraisals, and building projects. Dimensions, square footage, and floor plans are all part of the measuring process. Accuracy is achieved through the use of numerous techniques, such as valuations, floor layouts, and laser measuring machines.

Recognizing the building's overall form is the first step. The length and width of each space are recorded. The square footage of a property has a direct effect on its market value, so precise measurements are crucial. You can learn a lot about the house's potential and design by measuring things like ceiling height, door width, and window area.

Standardized methodologies are used by appraisers and real estate experts when measuring buildings to guarantee uniformity and fairness. These figures are critical in establishing the CMA strategy for valuing a property. The identification of comparable properties and the establishment of market values rely on accurate measurements.

Technology, such as laser measuring instruments and 3D modeling programs, has improved the precision of measurements. Distances may be measured instantly with laser technology, guaranteeing accuracy even in difficult environments. Buildings can now be better visualized and evaluated thanks to the use of 3D models created by trained professionals.

Accurately measuring a home or building is crucial not only for its value but also for any planned restorations, additions, or alterations and for guaranteeing conformity with local zoning ordinances. Professionals in the real estate industry who are skilled in taking accurate measurements of structures benefit their clients by increasing openness, helping them make well-informed decisions, and facilitating smooth transactions.

The Best Tools & Resources for Real Estate Math Calculations

Professionals in the modern real estate market have access to a wealth of materials that make mathematical calculations easier and more accurate. With these tools, professionals can quickly and accurately do difficult computations for their clients, resulting in better data for better decisions.

Mortgage payment, property valuation, and investment analysis calculators are just a few of the many that can be found online. Interest rates, loan terms, and property characteristics are just some of the variables that can be accounted for using these calculators.

Professionals can make their own specialized calculation templates using spreadsheet software like Microsoft Excel or Google Sheets. These systems provide tools for professionals to execute a wide range of real estate computations, while also retaining the versatility to address unique circumstances.

The real estate math problems can be solved with the help of mobile apps. Real estate professionals can now have immediate access to a wide variety of useful calculations, from mortgage calculators to property assessment tools, with the help of mobile applications.

Calculation needs in the real estate business have a comprehensive answer in the shape of software and platforms. These programs combine information, streamline routines, and house fundamental arithmetic in one place.

Training and tutorials on real estate math calculations are available from a variety of educational sites, both online and off. By utilizing these tools, experts will be able to deepen their understanding of mathematics and keep pace with developments in the field.

14.

Practice Questions

————•————

Chapter 1

What is the primary goal of the chapter "How to Pass the Exam"?

a) To provide information on different real estate markets

b) To teach advanced real estate investment strategies

c) To offer insights and strategies to excel in the licensing exam

d) To discuss the history of real estate laws

[Answer: c]

Which aspect of the exam does the chapter emphasize the most?

a) Memorization of specific facts and figures

b) Time management during the exam

c) Study strategies for general knowledge improvement

d) Techniques for overcoming fear of failure

[Answer: b]

Why is understanding the format and organization of the exam important?

a) It helps you avoid taking the test

b) It allows you to predict specific questions on the exam

c) It enables you to manage your time effectively during the exam

d) It guarantees a passing score regardless of preparation

[Answer: c]

Which of the following is NOT a part of efficient time management during the exam?

a) Taking a break after every question

b) Evaluating the difficulty of questions

c) Allocating appropriate time for each question

d) Identifying when to move on to the next question

[Answer: a]

What is the purpose of the "Test Tips" section?

a) To provide recommendations for passing real estate courses

b) To teach advanced investment strategies

c) To guide test-takers through the exam challenges and improve performance

d) To discuss historical aspects of real estate

[Answer: c]

Which strategy is NOT discussed in the section "Test Tips" for tackling different question types?

a) Reading questions carefully

b) Minimizing distractors

c) Randomly selecting an answer

d) Selecting the most appropriate response

[Answer: c]

What is the primary focus of the section "How To Overcome Test Anxiety"?

a) Exploring advanced real estate investment techniques

b) Overcoming anxiety related to exam preparation

c) Discussing legal aspects of real estate transactions

d) Providing historical context for real estate laws

[Answer: b]

Which practice helps to ground you in the present and combat anxiety?

a) Imagining future scenarios

b) Engaging in mindfulness practices

c) Ignoring your surroundings

d) Rushing through questions

[Answer: b]

What is the role of visualization in overcoming test anxiety?

a) It increases test anxiety

b) It helps you focus on hypothetical scenarios

c) It prepares your mind to take the test with confidence

d) It increases your knowledge of real estate laws

[Answer: c]

What is the main emphasis of the "Study Strategy" section?

a) Memorizing all real estate regulations

b) Focusing on passive learning strategies

c) Tailoring your study approach to improve learning and retention

d) Ignoring active learning methods

[Answer: c]

Why is creating an encouraging study environment important?

a) It doesn't impact study efficiency

b) It can lead to decreased concentration

c) It has no effect on anxiety levels

d) It can improve focus and concentration

[Answer: d]

Which aspect of preparation helps in reducing burnout?

a) Avoiding breaks

b) Maintaining a fast pace without pauses

c) Incorporating regular breaks

d) Working on study tasks for extended periods

[Answer: c]

What is the ultimate goal of the combined strategies discussed in the chapter?

a) Passing the exam with minimal effort

b) Establishing a foundation for a successful real estate career

c) Memorizing all real estate regulations

d) Avoiding the licensing exam altogether

[Answer: b]

What is the central message of the chapter's approach to exam preparation?

a) Memorization is the only effective strategy

b) One-size-fits-all study methods work for everyone

c) Active learning and strategic preparation are key to success

d) Anxiety is unavoidable and shouldn't be addressed

[Answer: c]

What does the chapter emphasize about the journey to obtaining a license?

a) Passing the exam is the sole goal

b) It's about developing skills and knowledge for a rewarding profession

c) Active learning strategies are unnecessary

d) Test-taking anxiety is inevitable and should be accepted

[Answer: b]

Chapter 2

What term refers to the legal entitlement to the airspace above a piece of property?

A) Mineral Rights

B) Water Rights

C) Air Rights

D) Easements

Answer: C

Which property ownership model involves complete control over a property's management and decisions?

A) Joint Tenancy

B) Tenancy in Common

C) Sole Ownership

D) Tenancy by the Entirety

Answer: C

In the Rectangular Government Survey System, what is the size of a township?

A) 1 square mile

B) 6 square miles

C) 36 square miles

D) 12 square miles

Answer: B

What type of encumbrance involves a legal claim on property as security for a debt or obligation?

A) Easement

B) Encroachment

C) Lien

D) License

Answer: C

What type of property rights allow the owner to extract minerals and resources from beneath the land's surface?

A) Air Rights

B) Water Rights

C) Mineral Rights

D) Easements

Answer: C

Which ownership structure allows spouses to have equal ownership and right of survivorship?

A) Joint Tenancy

B) Tenancy in Common

C) Tenancy by the Entirety

D) Sole Ownership

Answer: C

What term refers to legal descriptions that use actual measurements of a property's perimeter to establish boundaries?

A) Metes and Bounds

B) Lot-and-Block

C) Rectangular Government Survey

D) Property Description

Answer: A

Which type of encumbrance allows third parties the legal right to use a piece of land for their own benefit?

A) Lien

B) Encroachment

C) Easement

D) License

Answer: C

What is the main benefit of joint tenancy with right of survivorship?

A) Equal ownership shares

B) Freedom from property taxes

C) Protection from creditors

D) Automatic transfer of ownership upon death

Answer: D

What type of property ownership involves undivided interests and the absence of the right of survivorship?

A) Joint Tenancy

B) Tenancy in Common

C) Tenancy by the Entirety

D) Sole Ownership

Answer: B

What type of property ownership is characterized by assets acquired during a marriage being considered jointly owned?

A) Separate Property

B) Community Property

C) Sole Ownership

D) Joint Tenancy

Answer: B

What is the primary purpose of a lien on a property?

A) To allow the owner to build without restrictions

B) To establish a boundary between properties

C) To serve as security for a debt or obligation

D) To grant air rights to adjacent properties

Answer: C

Chapter 3

What does the chapter "Land Use Controls and Regulations" mainly focus on?

A) Property ownership

B) Real estate industry shifts

C) Governmental rights and restrictions

D) Historical preservation laws

Answer: C

What principle allows the government to seize private property for public use?

A) Zoning regulations

B) Eminent domain

C) Property ownership rights

D) Historical preservation laws

Answer: B

What governmental power enables the creation of laws promoting public safety, health, and welfare?

A) Property rights

B) Eminent domain

C) Police power

D) Zoning regulations

Answer: C

What is the primary goal of zoning regulations?

A) Promoting industrial use

B) Minimizing land use restrictions

C) Preventing incompatible land uses

D) Expanding urban sprawl

Answer: C

What is the purpose of building codes and regulations?

A) Encouraging reckless construction

B) Ensuring architectural creativity

C) Protecting safety and compliance

D) Promoting rapid construction

Answer: C

What do environmental regulations aim to achieve?

A) Ignoring ecological factors

B) Minimizing health concerns

C) Balancing individual property rights

D) Protecting natural resources and health

Answer: D

What type of sites undergo cleanup and remediation to make them suitable for redevelopment?

A) Greenfields

B) Bluefields

C) Brownfields

D) Redfields

Answer: C

What is the role of historical preservation in communities?

A) Demolishing historical sites

B) Ignoring cultural relevance

C) Celebrating architectural legacy

D) Excluding tourism opportunities

Answer: C

What mechanism allows property owners to request exceptions to zoning restrictions?

A) Variances

B) Easements

C) Deeds

D) Permits

Answer: A

What is the purpose of special use permits?

A) Allowing unrestricted land use

B) Promoting residential development

C) Restricting business operations

D) Permitting specific uses in certain zones

Answer: D

What governmental power enables the creation of laws promoting public safety, health, and welfare?

A) Property rights

B) Eminent domain

C) Police power

D) Zoning regulations

Answer: C

What is the primary goal of zoning regulations?

A) Promoting industrial use

B) Minimizing land use restrictions

C) Preventing incompatible land uses

D) Expanding urban sprawl

Answer: C

What is the purpose of building codes and regulations?

A) Encouraging reckless construction

B) Ensuring architectural creativity

C) Protecting safety and compliance

D) Promoting rapid construction

Answer: C

What do environmental regulations aim to achieve?

A) Ignoring ecological factors

B) Minimizing health concerns

C) Balancing individual property rights

D) Protecting natural resources and health

Answer: D

What type of sites undergo cleanup and remediation to make them suitable for redevelopment?

A) Greenfields

B) Bluefields

C) Brownfields

D) Redfields

Answer: C

Chapter 4

What is the primary purpose of an appraisal in real estate?

A) Marketing the property

B) Estimating value

C) Negotiating lease terms

D) Conducting property inspections

Answer: B

The principle that states a property's value is determined by the cost of acquiring a comparable substitute is known as:

A) Principle of anticipation

B) Principle of contribution

C) Principle of substitution

D) Principle of depreciation

Answer: C

The income analysis approach is particularly relevant for which type of properties?

A) Raw land

B) Historical landmarks

C) Income-generating properties

D) Luxury residences

Answer: C

What does the term "reconciliation" refer to in real estate appraisal?

A) Determining property location

B) Analyzing supply and demand

C) Evaluating various appraisal approaches

D) Assessing property depreciation

Answer: C

In a sellers' market, what is the likely impact on property prices?

A) Prices remain stable

B) Prices decrease

C) Prices increase

D) Prices fluctuate

Answer: C

What does ROI stand for in real estate investment analysis?

A) Rental Operation Investment

B) Return on Insurance

C) Return on Investment

D) Real Opportunity Income

Answer: C

The principle of substitution suggests that buyers:

A) Prefer unique properties

B) Will not pay more for a property than a comparable substitute

C) Only consider properties with the lowest price

D) Ignore market trends

Answer: B

The cost approach to valuation is particularly useful for valuing properties that are:

A) Common and easily replaceable

B) Income-generating properties

C) One-of-a-kind or specialized

D) In a buyer's market

Answer: C

What is the primary factor that determines whether a market is a buyers' or sellers' market?

A) Government regulations

B) Interest rates

C) Supply and demand dynamics

D) Property tax rates

Answer: C

Which economic principle underlies the concept that property features contribute disproportionately to its overall value?

A) Principle of contribution

B) Principle of anticipation

C) Principle of substitution

D) Principle of depreciation

Answer: A

W

hat does the Comparable Market Analysis (CMA) help real estate professionals determine?

A) Property tax rates

B) Mortgage interest rates

C) Rental income potential

D) Property values

Answer: D

The principle of anticipation in real estate refers to:

A) The principle of comparing market trends

B) Expectations of future benefits affecting value

C) Pricing properties based on their uniqueness

D) The principle of supply and demand

Answer: B

Which market condition is characterized by high demand and limited supply?

A) Sellers' market

B) Balanced market

C) Buyers' market

D) Neutral market

Answer: A

What is the primary purpose of reconciling different appraisal approaches?

A) To prove the accuracy of one specific approach

B) To adjust for inflation

C) To create confusion in the valuation process

D) To arrive at a comprehensive estimate of value

Answer: D

What is the significance of the capitalization rate (cap rate) in real estate investing?

A) It determines the mortgage interest rate

B) It influences property construction costs

C) It indicates the property's potential for rental income

D) It reflects the property's market value

Answer: C

Chapter 5

What is the purpose of the chapter on Financing in real estate?

A) Understanding property ownership

B) Exploring property types

C) Navigating financial complexities

D) Learning about property taxes

Answer: C

What term refers to the fees associated with taking out a loan to buy a home?

A) Interest rates

B) Down payment

C) Equity

D) Amortization

Answer: A

What impacts the total loan amount, monthly payments, and the need for PMI?

A) Interest rates

B) Down payment

C) Credit scores

D) Collateral

Answer: B

What is the purpose of amortization in real estate financing?

A) Increasing loan balance

B) Lowering interest rates

C) Building equity over time

D) Reducing loan term

Answer: C

What is the term for the difference between property value and the mortgage owed?

A) Equity

B) Interest

C) Collateral

D) Amortization

Answer: A

What is the function of collateral in real estate financing?

A) Setting interest rates

B) Reducing loan term

C) Providing security for loans

D) Calculating PITI

Answer: C

Which factor affects the interest rates offered by lenders?

A) Down payment

B) Credit scores

C) Loan term

D) Property taxes

Answer: B

What are escrow accounts used for in real estate transactions?

A) Paying off debt

B) Calculating equity

C) Holding funds for future expenses

D) Issuing mortgages

Answer: C

What is the main purpose of the underwriting process in real estate financing?

A) Determining interest rates

B) Evaluating credit scores

C) Assessing financial capabilities

D) Calculating amortization

Answer: C

What does LTV stand for in real estate financing?

A) Loan Term Value

B) Loan to Vendor

C) Loan-to-Value

D) Loan Total Value

Answer: C

What is Private Mortgage Insurance (PMI) used for?

A) Reducing interest rates

B) Protecting against financial loss

C) Lowering property taxes

D) Increasing credit scores

Answer: B

What does the DTI ratio measure in real estate financing?

A) Loan value to property value

B) Interest rate fluctuations

C) Income used for debt payments

D) Property appreciation

Answer: C

What does PITI stand for in mortgage payments?

A) Principal, Interest, Taxes, Inflation

B) Property, Insurance, Taxes, Interest

C) Principal, Inflation, Taxes, Income

D) Principal, Interest, Taxes, Insurance

Answer: D

What form of property ownership involves equal shares and right of survivorship?

A) Tenancy in common

B) Sole ownership

C) Joint tenancy

D) Tenancy by the entirety

Answer: C

What is the main role of pre-qualification in real estate financing?

A) Evaluating credit scores

B) Providing a loan commitment

C) Analyzing debt-to-income ratio

D) Determining initial loan eligibility

Answer: D

Chapter 6

What is the main difference between agency relationships and non-agency relationships?

A) Agency relationships involve comprehensive advocacy.

B) Non-agency relationships prioritize fiduciary duties.

C) Both agency and non-agency provide equal representation.

D) Agency relationships focus on minimal assistance.

Answer: A

What is the main responsibility of agents towards their clients?

A) Provide minimal aid during transactions.

B) Prioritize the interests of customers.

C) Advocate for the best interests of clients.

D) Act as intermediaries between buyers and sellers.

Answer: C

Which party in a real estate transaction conducts deals without being represented by an agent?

A) Clients

B) Customers

C) Consumers

D) Brokers

Answer: C

What is the role of a buyer's agent?

A) Represent the seller's interests.

B) Promote and sell properties on behalf of sellers.

C) Advocate for the buyer throughout the buying process.

D) Balance the interests of both buyer and seller.

Answer: C

What is the main purpose of agency disclosure laws?

A) Protect the interests of agents.

B) Ensure confidentiality in transactions.

C) Promote dual agency relationships.

D) Provide transparency about agency relationships.

Answer: D

What is the purpose of listing agreements?

A) Promote a property to potential buyers.

B) Establish exclusive buyer representation.

C) Define the duties of a dual agent.

D) Determine the commission for non-exclusive agents.

Answer: A

What does a buyer agency agreement establish?

A) Seller's responsibilities in marketing the property.

B) Exclusive representation of the buyer by the agent.

C) Listing price of the property.

D) Legal ownership of the property.

Answer: B

In a dual agency, what is the potential challenge for agents?

A) Reduced efficiency in communication.

B) Struggle to find potential buyers.

C) Managing conflicts of interest.

D) Ensuring buyer exclusivity.

Answer: C

What is the primary duty of agents in a non-exclusive buyer agency agreement?

A) Advocating for the best interests of the buyer.

B) Negotiating offers on behalf of the seller.

C) Providing comprehensive representation to the buyer.

D) Collaborating with multiple buyers simultaneously.

Answer: A

What is the main role of a broker in the real estate industry?

A) Represent buyers and sellers in transactions.

B) Assist clients with property searches.

C) Manage a team of real estate agents.

D) Focus on marketing and property promotion.

Answer: C

What is the primary purpose of agency disclosure laws?

A) To regulate commission fees.

B) To promote dual agency relationships.

C) To ensure transparency about agency relationships.

D) To enforce exclusive representation agreements.

Answer: C

What is the difference between exclusive and non-exclusive buyer agency agreements?

A) Exclusive agreements allow buyers to work with multiple agents.

B) Non-exclusive agreements restrict buyers to a single agent.

C) Both agreements offer the same level of representation.

D) Exclusive agreements restrict buyers to one property.

Answer: A

What is the significance of an agency agreement in real estate transactions?

A) It determines the property's listing price.

B) It outlines the responsibilities of both parties.

C) It guarantees a successful sale.

D) It simplifies the process of property transfer.

Answer: B

What is the potential benefit of a dual agency in a real estate transaction?

A) Simplified communication between parties.

B) Enhanced confidentiality for buyers and sellers.

C) Guaranteed higher selling price for the property.

D) Elimination of potential conflicts of interest.

Answer: A

What is the main responsibility of agents in non-agency relationships?

A) Advocate for clients' best interests.

B) Provide comprehensive representation.

C) Offer minimal assistance and information.

D) Ensure fiduciary duties are upheld.

Answer: C

Chapter 7

What is the purpose of property disclosures in real estate transactions?

A) To increase property value

B) To create secrecy between buyers and sellers

C) To provide transparency and information to buyers

D) To reduce legal responsibilities for sellers

Answer: C

What does a property survey typically include?

A) Listing prices of neighboring properties

B) Physical characteristics of a property's interior

C) Map with property boundaries and legal details

D) Property's historical sales data

Answer: C

What is the purpose of required property disclosures?

A) To make buyers pay more for the property

B) To protect buyers from hidden property issues

C) To keep sellers' information private

D) To make negotiations more complicated

Answer: B

Which of the following is NOT an area typically covered in property disclosures?

A) Structural defects

B) Recent maintenance or improvements

C) Current market trends

D) Environmental hazards

Answer: C

What are the potential consequences for sellers who fail to provide accurate property disclosures?

A) Higher property value

B) Enhanced reputation among buyers

C) Legal actions, fines, and damage to reputation

D) Lower chances of litigation

Answer: C

What is the importance of transparency in property disclosures?

A) It increases property taxes

B) It creates confusion for buyers

C) It fosters trust and informed decision-making

D) It discourages negotiations

Answer: C

What term refers to the deliberate act of hiding material information about a property?

A) Transparency

B) Disclosure

C) Concealment

D) Enhancement

Answer: C

What is the potential outcome if a buyer discovers undisclosed flaws after purchasing a property?

A) The buyer is responsible for all repairs

B) The buyer can claim a refund of the purchase price

C) The buyer must accept the property as-is

D) The buyer forfeits their right to legal action

Answer: B

What legal consequences can sellers face for inadequate disclosures?

A) A higher selling price

B) Regulatory awards

C) Legal fees and potential damages

D) Exemption from disclosure requirements

Answer: C

Why is it important for buyers to conduct their own inspections?

A) To increase the purchase price

B) To save time during the transaction

C) To avoid legal consequences

D) To verify information provided in disclosures

Answer: D

Chapter 8

What is the fundamental concept that underlies all legitimate contracts?

A) Offer

B) Consideration

C) Mutual assent

D) Acceptance

Answer: C

Which of the following can transform a simple promise into a legally binding contract?

A) Verbal agreement

B) Competent parties

C) Mutual disagreement

D) Future consideration

Answer: B

Contracts that are not enforceable due to legal or procedural grounds are considered:

A) Void contracts

B) Voidable contracts

C) Unenforceable contracts

D) Valid contracts

Answer: C

What is the first step that leads to a legally binding contract?

A) Consideration

B) Acceptance

C) Offer

D) Intent

Answer: C

Which legal principle defines an agreement made free of coercion or undue influence?

A) Capacity

B) Acceptance

C) Consideration

D) Mutual assent

Answer: D

What is the main purpose of an addendum in a contract?

A) To terminate the contract

B) To modify the contract terms

C) To declare the contract void

D) To create a new contract

Answer: B

A contract that has no legal effect from the beginning is referred to as:

A) Void

B) Voidable

C) Unenforceable

D) Valid

Answer: A

What is the purpose of an option agreement in real estate?

A) To finalize the transaction

B) To modify contract terms

C) To grant the right to buy or sell

D) To cancel a contract

Answer: C

In a lease agreement, who are the parties involved?

A) Buyer and seller

B) Lessor and lessee

C) Landlord and tenant

D) Offeror and offeree

Answer: C

Which component is necessary to ensure mutual assent in a contract?

A) Consideration

B) Acceptance

C) Capacity

D) Offer

Answer: B

What is the purpose of a listing agreement in real estate?

A) To finalize the sale

B) To establish property ownership

C) To modify the contract

D) To market and sell the property

Answer: D

A contract that can be voided if certain conditions are met is known as:

A) Void contract

B) Voidable contract

C) Unenforceable contract

D) Executed contract

Answer: B

What is the main purpose of an assignment contract in real estate?

A) To finalize the sale

B) To modify the contract

C) To transfer contract rights and obligations

D) To terminate the contract

Answer: C

What is the primary requirement for a contract to be valid?

A) Mutual assent

B) Monetary compensation

C) Verbal agreement

D) Electronic signature

Answer: A

What is the role of consideration in a contract?

A) It guarantees mutual assent

B) It determines the validity of the contract

C) It ensures both parties have something at stake

D) It finalizes the acceptance process

Answer: C

Chapter 9

What is the primary advantage of leasing compared to property ownership?

A) Long-term responsibilities

B) Lack of options

C) Higher costs

D) Ownership rights

Answer: A

Which type of lease agreement is tailored for non-residential uses?

A) Residential Lease Agreement

B) Commercial Lease Agreement

C) Subletting Lease Agreement

D) Renewal Lease Agreement

Answer: B

What is the purpose of a security deposit in a lease agreement?

A) To cover the tenant's utility bills

B) To cover the landlord's property taxes

C) To cover any potential damages or rent nonpayment

D) To pay for lease renewal fees

Answer: C

Which aspect of a lease agreement specifies the permitted use of the rented space?

A) Lease Term

B) Rent Payment

C) Maintenance Responsibilities

D) Use and Occupancy

Answer: D

In a commercial lease, what are the three main types of lease structures?

A) Gross, Moderate, and Net leases

B) Gross, Net, and Standard leases

C) Gross, Modified Gross, and Net leases

D) Gross, Basic, and Advanced leases

Answer: C

What is the primary goal of lease renewals?

A) Increasing the rent dramatically

B) Terminating the lease early

C) Adjusting the lease terms for the tenant's benefit

D) Extending the lease for another term

Answer: D

How are lease terms affected when a property is sold to a new owner?

A) The lease terms are automatically voided.

B) The tenant's rights and obligations remain unchanged.

C) The tenant's rights are revoked, but their obligations remain.

D) Both the tenant's and landlord's rights are reset.

Answer: B

What is the most common cause of eviction?

A) Expiration of lease term

B) Non-compliance with lease conditions

C) Tenant's failure to pay rent

D) Landlord's desire for renovation

Answer: C

What is the purpose of a termination clause in a lease agreement?

A) To set the rent amount

B) To describe the property in detail

C) To outline repair responsibilities

D) To specify the procedures for ending the lease

Answer: D

Which party is responsible for maintaining a habitable property in a lease agreement?

A) Tenant

B) Landlord

C) Property manager

D) Neighbors

Answer: B

What is the primary objective of an eviction process?

A) To increase the rent amount

B) To end a lease peacefully

C) To regain ownership of the property

D) To extend the lease duration

Answer: C

Which element of a lease agreement specifies the specific address and features of the rented property?

A) Lease Term

B) Rent Payment

C) Premises Description

D) Repairs and Upkeep

Answer: C

What must landlords provide to tenants regarding the presence of lead-based paint?

A) A warning about pet allergies

B) A notification about nearby schools

C) Information about rent payment methods

D) Disclosure about the presence of lead-based paint

Answer: D

What is the primary responsibility of tenants in a lease agreement?

A) Collecting rent from other tenants

B) Ensuring the property is habitable

C) Selling the property when needed

D) Conducting repairs and maintenance

Answer: B

What is the purpose of a security deposit in a lease agreement?

A) It covers the landlord's taxes

B) It acts as the final month's rent

C) It provides a cushion for potential damages

D) It guarantees lease renewal

Answer: C

Chapter 10

What is the primary goal of property management?

A) Maximizing tenant disputes

B) Decreasing property value

C) Generating profits and preserving property value

D) Avoiding tenant interaction

Answer: C

What are property management agreements?

A) Tenant agreements

B) Landlord agreements

C) Agreements between property owners and property management entities

D) Agreements between tenants and property managers

Answer: C

What is the role of property managers in maintaining property value?

A) Ignoring maintenance to save costs

B) Decreasing tenant satisfaction

C) Regular maintenance and repairs to preserve value

D) Disregarding tenant concerns

Answer: C

What does "maintenance" refer to in property management?

A) Regular tenant inspections

B) Responding to repair requests

C) Preventive measures to keep property in good condition

D) Property owner's responsibilities

Answer: C

What is the importance of open communication in landlord-tenant relationships?

A) It is not necessary for a successful relationship

B) It helps escalate conflicts

C) It fosters tenant happiness and prevents issues from worsening

D) It's only beneficial for property owners

Answer: C

What is one responsibility of property managers in dispute resolution?

A) Ignoring tenant concerns

B) Quick resolution of conflicts

C) Blaming tenants for conflicts

D) Avoiding conflict resolution altogether

Answer: B

What is the purpose of an operating account in property management?

A) To hold security deposits

B) To manage maintenance expenses

C) To collect rent payments

D) To generate profits

Answer: B

Which laws prohibit discrimination in housing transactions?

A) Rent control laws

B) Property management laws

C) Fair housing laws

D) Lease agreement laws

Answer: C

What does "fair housing laws" aim to prevent?

A) Rent increases

B) Discrimination in housing transactions

C) Tenant disputes

D) Maintenance issues

Answer: B

What does tenant screening involve in property management?

A) Screening potential landlords

B) Evaluating credit and contacting references

C) Discriminating against certain tenants

D) Inspecting property value

Answer: B

What is the primary role of property managers in financial management?

A) Avoiding financial records

B) Generating profits for themselves

C) Ensuring accurate financial reporting and budgeting

D) Hiding expenses from property owners

Answer: C

How do property managers contribute to tenant retention?

A) By ignoring maintenance requests

B) Through regular maintenance and quick repairs

C) By increasing rent prices

D) By evicting tenants frequently

Answer: B

What is the purpose of "reasonable accommodations" for disabled tenants?

A) To increase rent prices

B) To minimize tenant interactions

C) To improve property value

D) To enhance accessibility for disabled tenants

Answer: D

What does fair housing training for property managers involve?

A) Ignoring fair housing laws

B) Keeping documents related to tenant disputes

C) Complying with fair housing rules and regulations

D) Discriminating against certain tenants

Answer: C

What do property management agreements ensure?

A) Transparency, responsibility, and professionalism

B) Exclusivity for property owners

C) Avoidance of maintenance and repairs

D) Disregard for tenant concerns

Answer: A

Chapter 11

What is the primary purpose of a deed in real estate transactions?

A) Ensure property maintenance

B) Transfer ownership legally

C) Provide title insurance

D) Determine property value

Answer: B

Which type of deed offers the greatest protection to the grantee?

A) General warranty deed

B) Special warranty deed

C) Quitclaim deed

D) Bargain and sale deed

Answer: A

What does a "cloud on title" refer to?

A) A weather-related issue with the property

B) A claim, lien, or encumbrance affecting ownership

C) A legal dispute over property value

D) A type of property deed

Answer: B

What does a title search aim to uncover?

A) Current property owners

B) Market value of the property

C) History of property ownership and potential issues

D) Zoning regulations

Answer: C

What is the purpose of title insurance?

A) Protects against weather-related damages

B) Provides guarantees for a clear title

C) Covers property maintenance costs

D) Determines property boundaries

Answer: B

What does a quiet title action aim to achieve?

A) Remove liens from the property

B) Speed up the title transfer process

C) Clear any claims to the property's ownership

D) Change property boundaries

Answer: C

What is the main distinction between marketable and insurable titles?

A) Marketable titles are more appealing to buyers

B) Marketable titles satisfy title insurance requirements

C) Insurable titles are claim-free

D) Insurable titles are guaranteed by the grantor

Answer: B

What is the primary purpose of an owner's title insurance?

A) Protects the grantor's interests

B) Provides guarantees for a clear title

C) Protects the lender's interests

D) Ensures property maintenance

Answer: B

What is a key component required for a valid deed?

A) A high market value of the property

B) Grantor's financial stability

C) A complete history of property owners

D) Intent of the grantor to transfer ownership

Answer: D

Which type of deed conveys the grantor's interest without any guarantees?

A) General warranty deed

B) Special warranty deed

C) Quitclaim deed

D) Bargain and sale deed

Answer: C

What is the purpose of a title search in property transactions?

A) Determine the property's current market value

B) Uncover potential issues with the property's ownership history

C) Verify the grantor's financial stability

D) Investigate the property's construction quality

Answer: B

What does a special warranty deed protect the grantee against?

A) Claims from prior owners

B) Claims that arise during the grantor's possession

C) Encumbrances on the property

D) Any defects in the property's physical condition

Answer: B

What does a quitclaim deed convey to the grantee?

A) A guarantee of clear title

B) The grantor's entire interest in the property

C) The grantor's financial stability

D) A promise to pay the grantee a sum of money

Answer: B

What is the primary purpose of a quiet title action?

A) To speed up the title transfer process

B) To challenge the validity of the grantee's ownership

C) To clear any claims to the property's ownership

D) To determine property boundaries

Answer: C

What is the significance of having a marketable title?

A) It guarantees a claim-free title

B) It makes the property more attractive to buyers

C) It satisfies the requirements for title insurance

D) It allows the grantor to transfer the property without consent

Answer: B

Chapter 12

Effective communication in real estate involves:

A) Only talking to clients

B) Adjusting communication styles

C) Ignoring client feedback

D) Avoiding emotional connections

Answer: B

What is the main purpose of escrow and trust accounts in real estate?

A) Maximizing agent profits

B) Transparent management of client finances

C) Personal use of client funds

D) Investment opportunities for agents

Answer: B

Which of the following practices is prohibited in real estate due to discrimination concerns?

A) Blockbusting

B) Customer profiling

C) Direct marketing

D) Location-based discounts

Answer: A

Fair housing laws protect against discrimination based on:

A) Income levels

B) Pet ownership

C) National origin

D) Communication preferences

Answer: C

What do blockbusting, steering, and redlining have in common?

A) They encourage diversity in housing

B) They are permitted under fair housing laws

C) They perpetuate bias and discrimination

D) They promote transparency in real estate

Answer: C

What is the primary goal of real estate negotiation?

A) Favoring the agent's interests

B) Achieving a win-win agreement

C) Dominating the other party

D) Rushing to close the deal

Answer: B

How has technology impacted the real estate industry?

A) Decreased client engagement

B) Replaced the need for real estate professionals

C) Streamlined operations and improved customer experience

D) Eliminated the need for negotiation

Answer: C

Ethical considerations in real estate emphasize:

A) Maximizing profits at any cost

B) Following laws only when necessary

C) Transparency, client interests, and credibility

D) Promoting bias and discrimination

Answer: C

Different employment models for real estate agents:

A) Offer the same benefits and responsibilities

B) Do not impact the way they do their jobs

C) Come with distinct benefits and obligations

D) Are solely determined by the clients

Answer: C

Due diligence in real estate involves:

A) Ignoring property history and zoning laws

B) Focusing only on financial aspects

C) Educating clients about property details and laws

D) Neglecting professional assistance

Answer: C

A buyer's agent in real estate is responsible for:

A) Representing the seller's interests

B) Negotiating contracts for both parties

C) Advocating for the buyer's interests

D) Managing trust and escrow accounts

Answer: C

The antitrust laws in real estate aim to:

A) Promote cooperation between agents

B) Prevent fair competition

C) Encourage anti-competitive practices

D) Ensure fair and competitive market practices

Answer: D

What is the primary focus of fair housing laws?

A) Encouraging property ownership for investors

B) Protecting agents' interests

C) Preventing discrimination in housing

D) Expanding housing options for pets

Answer: C

How does effective communication help in real estate?

A) By only providing information to clients

B) By building trust and understanding

C) By avoiding any emotional connections

D) By focusing solely on digital communication

Answer: B

What is the role of transaction coordinators in real estate?

A) Handling property valuations

B) Negotiating contracts

C) Managing trust and escrow accounts

D) Overseeing paperwork and timelines

Answer: D

Chapter 13

Real estate calculations are crucial for making informed decisions related to:

A) Architecture and design

B) Property advertising

C) Transactions and valuations

D) Digital marketing strategies

Answer: C

Which mathematical operations serve as the basis for more intricate real estate computations?

A) Square roots and exponents

B) Addition and subtraction

C) Multiplication and division

D) Trigonometric functions

Answer: B

What is the T-Bar Method used for in real estate calculations?

A) Calculating area of land

B) Converting fractions to decimals

C) Organizing and solving complex problems

D) Analyzing property appreciation

Answer: C

Why is the ability to convert between percentages, decimals, and fractions important in real estate?

A) It makes calculations more complicated

B) It improves data visualization

C) It helps with architectural design

D) It aids in accurate property valuations

Answer: D

The PITI formula in mortgage payment calculations includes:

A) Principal, interest, taxes, investment

B) Price, insurance, taxes, interest

C) Principal, interest, taxes, insurance

D) Payment, interest, taxes, investment

Answer: C

Which approach to property valuation involves analyzing comparable property sales?

A) Revenue Approach

B) Cost Approach

C) Comparative Market Analysis

D) Income Approach

Answer: C

Transfer taxes are collected when:

A) A property is rented out

B) A property is being appraised

C) Ownership of a property is transferred

D) A property undergoes renovations

Answer: C

The cash-on-cash return in real estate investment analysis is a measure of:

A) Rental income minus expenses

B) Property appreciation over time

C) Initial return on investment

D) Total profitability of the property

Answer: C

Capitalization rate (cap rate) and Gross Rent Multiplier (GRM) are important for:

A) Calculating property taxes

B) Estimating closing costs

C) Analyzing investment opportunities

D) Determining land measurements

Answer: C

What are buyer funds in a real estate transaction?

A) Funds used for interior design

B) Financial resources needed to close the deal

C) Funds provided by the seller

D) Rental income from the property

Answer: B

What are seller proceeds in a real estate transaction?

A) Additional fees for the buyer

B) The costs of home improvements

C) Funds retained by the buyer

D) The amount left over for the seller after expenses

Answer: D

Equity in real estate is calculated as the difference between:

A) Mortgage balance and purchase price

B) Property taxes and insurance costs

C) Current market value and property size

D) Down payment and mortgage interest

Answer: A

What does the term "depreciation" refer to in real estate?

A) An increase in property value over time

B) The amount paid to the real estate agent

C) The reduction in taxable income over time

D) The appreciation of rental income

Answer: C

Accurate land measurement is essential for:

A) Designing property advertisements

B) Calculating property taxes

C) Valuation of properties and zoning adherence

D) Determining rental income

Answer: C

What is the purpose of using 3D modeling programs in measuring structures?

A) Designing architectural plans

B) Enhancing property advertisements

C) Facilitating virtual tours for clients

D) Improving the accuracy of measurements

Answer: D

Made in the USA
Las Vegas, NV
25 November 2023

81519967R00103